Battleships of
the World

The early research for this book was carried out while I held a Schoolmaster Fellowship at St Martin's College, Lancaster (now the University of Cumbria).

My thanks go to the Governors of the College, and of Lancaster Royal Grammar School, for enabling me to do this.

Battleships of the World

Struggle for Naval Supremacy
1820–1945

John Fidler

Pen & Sword
MARITIME

First published in Great Britain in 2016 by
Pen & Sword Maritime
an imprint of
Pen & Sword Books Ltd
47 Church Street
Barnsley
South Yorkshire
S70 2AS

ISBN 978 1 47387 146 5

A CIP catalogue record for this book is available from the British
Library

Typeset in Ehrhardt by
Mac Style Ltd, Bridlington, East Yorkshire
Printed and bound in the UK by CPI Group (UK) Ltd,
Croydon, CRO 4YY

Pen & Sword Books Ltd incorporates the imprints of Pen & Sword
Archaeology, Atlas, Aviation, Battleground, Discovery, Family
History, History, Maritime, Military, Naval, Politics, Railways,
Select, Transport, True Crime, and Fiction, Frontline Books, Leo
Cooper, Praetorian Press, Seaforth Publishing and Wharncliffe.

For a complete list of Pen & Sword titles please contact
PEN & SWORD BOOKS LIMITED
47 Church Street, Barnsley, South Yorkshire, S70 2AS, England
E-mail: enquiries@pen-and-sword.co.uk
Website: www.pen-and-sword.co.uk

Contents

Introduction

The battle squadrons of the Royal Navy, assembled at Spithead for the Naval Review of 1914, epitomised the armoured battleship at the height of its prestige. The long columns of majestic vessels represented Britain's long-held mastery of the sea which had enabled the building of an empire, the defeat of Napoleon and the commercial supremacy of the past century.

The very names of the ships emphasised the traditions of the service: *Ajax*, *Neptune*, *Conqueror*, *Orion*, *Colossus* and *Thunderer* were all named after ships which had fought in the battle line at Trafalgar. An *Audacious* had fought at Aboukir Bay (the Battle of the Nile), where a *Vanguard* had been Nelson's flagship, while another *Vanguard* and a *Hercules* had fought the Armada. There had been a *Monarch* at Copenhagen, a *Superb* at Algeciras. A *Centurion* had been Anson's flagship for his epic voyage around the world and a *Bellerophon* had seen the surrender of Napoleon.

Now all of these names were borne by massive armoured ships, armed with guns of at least 12-inch calibre, any one of which could have reduced to matchwood an entire fleet of Nelson's day. Among vessels nearing completion were a *Royal Sovereign*, a *Warspite* and a *Revenge*, inheritors of some of the most famous names, while the most famous of all *Victory*, launched in 1765, was then still afloat in Portsmouth harbour.

Dreadnought herself was named after a ship which had been in Drake's squadron in Cadiz in 1587 and in Howard's fleet in the Channel the following year. A second ship of the name had fought in the Dutch

HMS *Victory*, afloat in Portsmouth harbour.

wars of the seventeenth century, a third against the French at Barfleur and Cape Passaro. Yet another had been Collingwood's flagship in the blockade of Cadiz in 1805 and had fought at Trafalgar. Now the name was given to a new generation of fast, powerful armoured battleships. In 1914 the expectation was that the great issues of the war at sea would still be decided, as they had been for some four centuries, by the battle fleets. That certainty was shaken by the inconclusive nature of the gun duel at Jutland and by the vulnerability of the great ships to mine and torpedo. Finally, it was to be shattered by the aircraft which wrought such destruction at Taranto and Pearl Harbor, which sank Force Z and eventually overwhelmed the Japanese leviathans *Yamato* and *Musashi*. By 1945 it was clear that the end of the battleship era had come and the great ships, which were scrapped in the aftermath of the Second World War, were not replaced.

Chapter One

The Age of Innovation 1820–1870

The great three-decked ships of the line of the early nineteenth century were still in the direct line of development from the *Revenge* of 1577. The *Royal Sovereign* of 1642, the *Victory* of 1765 and the 120-gun *Caledonia* of 1808, despite the technical improvements in ship design, all had essential features in common. They were wooden-built, dependent on wind and sail, and were armed with broadside-mounted, muzzle loading guns firing solid shot. The revolution in ship design in the mid-nineteenth century saw the advent of iron and steel construction and armour, steam power and turret-mounted breech-loading guns firing explosive shells. All of these innovations were greeted with a good deal of caution, and each posed considerable technical problems, but in total they transformed the world's fighting navies in a generation.

Although steam power conferred the immense advantage of independence from the wind, it suffered from massive drawbacks. Engines were prone to breaking down in the early years. Aboard a wooden warship even the galley fire was a hazard and boiler rooms seemed terribly vulnerable to gunfire; paddle wheels were similarly vulnerable and even more exposed. Moreover the rate of consumption of coal meant that no vessel intended for the open sea could be solely dependent on her engines. However, by the 1820s, the navies of France, Britain and the USA were among those using steam paddle tugs for harbour work. Experiments with the far more efficient screw propeller were made in the following decades, with the Americans launching the first screw warship in 1843, the 10-gun sloop *Princeton*. Two years later

The duel between *Rattler* and *Alecto*.

the Admiralty staged the famous duel in which the screw sloop *Rattler* was lashed stern to stern with the paddle steamer *Alecto*, of similar size and power, in a tug-of-war. *Alecto* suffered the indignity of being dragged backwards, while at full power, at almost three knots.

The screw frigate *Ajax* was the first of a series of warships to be built as a result and by 1850 screw propulsion was being applied to first-rates, the 90-gun *Agamemnon* among them, while existing ships were converted to steam.

However, for the next twenty years steam was regarded as providing auxiliary power only and a full sailing rig was an essential part of any warship. Moreover, an emphasis on sail-drill and seamanship as the priority, at times hindered development.

The use of the explosive shell was not unknown in naval warfare in the eighteenth century. The ungainly bomb-ketches of the time mounted one or two mortars amidships, the whole vessel having to be aligned in the direction of fire. The explosive was detonated by a

HMS *Agamemnon*.

fuse of slow match, lit before the propellant charge of gunpowder was
fired. This was not only a hazardous operation aboard a wooden ship,
but the rate of burning of the fuse was unreliable. Resulting accidents
suggested that the shell was not really suited to naval warfare until, in
1824, the invention of a French artillery officer solved the problem.
Colonel Henri-Joseph Paixhans tested a shell-firing gun in which the
fuse of the shell was lit by the flash of the propellant, so that until the
gun was fired, the shell was safe.

Around the same time came experiments with breech loading and
with rifling, to improve accuracy, but difficulties with the construction
of a reliable breech mechanism led the Royal Navy to the continued
reliance on muzzle-loaders until 1879. Then an accident occurred
when a 38-ton muzzle-loader in *Thunderer* burst. It was discovered
that the gun which had misfired, had been reloaded again by mistake
and that the double charge had shattered the barrel. Muzzle-loaders
of the time were reloaded by being depressed in line with angled

reloading tubes set in the deck, with the charges and shells inserted by a hydraulic ram. The noise had been so deafening that the gun crew had failed to realise that one gun had misfired. Such an error would, of course, be impossible in a breech-loaded gun.

Guns of this size and larger (a 100-ton gun was produced by Armstrongs in 1876) could not be carried in large numbers by the wooden ships of the line, so a form of mounting had to be devised to bring the main armament to bear on either broadside. Guns were either mounted in a revolving turret, or on a turntable behind an armoured barbette; the first experiments with turret-ships were made in the 1860s.

Armour was clearly vital for protection from shell-firing guns: the destruction of an unarmoured Turkish squadron by the Russians at Sinope in the Black Sea in 1853 was proof of this, if proof were needed. The earliest ironclads were simply wooden ships fitted with an armoured belt, though it must be remembered that by 1820 such vessels also had ribs of iron. The first ironclad was the French *Gloire*, a two-decked screw vessel cut down to a single gun deck and given a simpler sail rig and armour in 1853. Two sister vessels were similarly altered and a fourth ship, *Couronne*, was laid down. These singularly ugly ships stirred the Admiralty into action and in 1859 the first

HMS *Warrior*.

British ironclad, *Warrior*, was laid down. Along with her half-sister *Black Prince* and *Couronne*, she was the first iron battleship, although classed as a frigate since she had only one gun deck.

Of 9,200 tons displacement, *Warrior* was the largest ship then built, was capable of 14 knots and mounted thirty-two muzzle-loaders on the broadside. Reclassified as an armoured cruiser in 1867, she and *Black Prince* were placed in reserve in 1871 and then withdrawn from service in 1883. *Black Prince* saw service as a training ship before being scrapped in 1923, but *Warrior* survives. She became part of the Navy's Torpedo Establishment at Portsmouth in 1904 as *Vernon III*,

Figurehead of HMS *Warrior*.

Oil hulk.

her own name being transferred to a new armoured cruiser. Twenty-five years later she was towed to Pembroke Dock at Milford Haven where she served for fifty years as an oil jetty under the inglorious name Oil Fuel Hulk C77. With her deck concreted over and a line of huts and street lamps along it, she refuelled over 5,000 ships in these

CSS *Virginia* (ex-*Merrimack*).

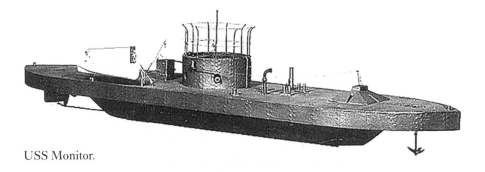

USS Monitor.

years, before restoration became an issue. Ownership was transferred to the Maritime Trust in 1979 and she was towed to Hartlepool for the work to be carried out. Restored, she was towed to Portsmouth in 1987, where she still dominates the harbour.

By 1862 then, the three innovations of steam power, armour and shell-firing guns had been accepted as the basis of naval design. But

Battle of Hampton Roads.

apart from some minor actions, there had been no battle to test the new ships. Neither the British nor the French navies saw action in the 1860s, but the Americans had been well abreast of naval developments and were fighting their Civil War. Here the Confederate States, in possession of the Navy Yard at Norfolk, Virginia, set to work on the hulk of the steam frigate *Merrimack*. In dock for an engine overhaul, she had been set on fire and scuttled by her Union officers on the outbreak of war. Now salvaged, she was cut down almost to the waterline and a long, sloping casemate of timber, faced with four inches of railway iron was built. This was pierced with ten gun ports and the vessel, renamed *Virginia*, set out to attack the Union shipping in Hampton Roads. She sank the 24-gun sloop *Cumberland* and forced the 44-gun frigate *Congress* with her sisters *Minnesota* and *Roanoake* to run aground.

At nightfall there arrived off Hampton Roads one of the strangest vessels ever seen. The Union's response to the conversion of the *Merrimack* had been the rapid construction of the *Monitor* to the design of the Swede John Ericsson. A shallow-draught hull was provided with an armoured deck, a conning tower and a centrally-mounted turret housing two 11-inch smooth-bore guns. Aptly described as 'a cheese-box on a raft', she had struggled down from New York, so that when *Virginia* emerged to complete her work of destruction, she faced another ironclad. Their gun duel was something of an anti-climax. The defensive armour of each vessel far outclassed the hitting-power of their guns as the two manoeuvred ponderously and fired even more slowly, breaking off the action after three hours.

The effect of this action upon naval construction was remarkable and immediate. Not only did the Union decide that the future lay in turreted 'monitors' (the name became generic, though the name-vessel foundered in a heavy sea off Cape Hatteras, North Carolina in 1862) but the European powers began to build to this design. The Admiralty breastwork monitor *Glatton* of 1872 was typical of the French and

Italian ram *Affondatore*.

HMS *Hotspur* with anti-torpedo net deployed.

British examples, but the Russians built two monitors of circular hull-form. By this time, however, another lesson of modern warfare had apparently been taught by the Battle of Lissa, in the Adriatic, in 1866. This was the use of the ram – a revival of the battle tactics of the galley. A ship with its own motive power, whether oars or steam, might well inflict mortal damage by ramming, and the Italians commissioned the *Affondatore* in 1866. Built at Milwall, she displaced 4,000 tons and was armed with two turret-mounted guns, but had as her main offensive weapon a fearsome 26-foot ram.

At Lissa, she failed to inflict any damage on her opponents, but the Austrian flagship *Erzherzog Ferdinand Max* did sink the *Re d'Italia* by ramming.

The British turret-ram *Hotspur* was designed in 1868 on the assumption that 'the ram, and the ram only, need be feared at sea', the lack of success of the purpose-built *Affondatore* being conveniently overlooked. The *Polyphemus* was originally laid down in 1882 as a

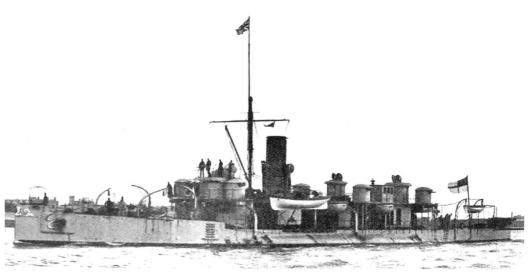

Torpedo ram warship HMS Polyphemus.

HMS *Victoria*.

ram without any other offensive armament, but was completed as a
torpedo-ram in an attempt to blend another innovation into the pattern
of development. None of these craft had any success in action, though
one finds an interesting fictional example in H.G. Wells's *The War of
the Worlds* in the destruction of a Martian fighting machine by the
'torpedo-ram Thunder Child'.

   That the ram could be a formidable weapon – albeit in peacetime
and against consorts – was proved by frequent accidents. Ships of the
Russian, French, German and Spanish navies were lost to ramming
during manoeuvres, while the Royal Navy lost *Vanguard* in 1875
(rammed by *Iron Duke*) and, even more famously Admiral Tryon's
flagship *Victoria*, rammed by *Camperdown* in the Gulf of Sirte in the
Mediterranean in 1888.

   The early turreted monitors were all essentially coastal defence or
bombardment vessels, too slow and unseaworthy to work with a fleet

HMS *Captain*.

in the open sea. In 1864 the Admiralty laid down its first turret ship, *Prince Albert*, and had begun the conversion of the three-decker *Royal Sovereign* into another. Each carried four guns in turrets mounted on the centre-line, but they too were coastal defence ships. In the plans for a sea-going equivalent the insistence of the Admiralty on a full sailing rig and a high freeboard led to a most unsatisfactory compromise in design. The very weight of the turret meant that it could not be carried high above the water-line without adversely affecting the ship's mobility, while the rigging masked the all-round fire of the guns. *Monarch* was laid down in the Admiralty dockyard at Chatham in 1866 and was completed three years later. Her main armament of four 12-inch guns was carried in two paired turrets amidships, limiting their use as there was no possibility of end-on fire. She displaced 8,300 tons and had a freeboard amidships of 14 feet, with an armoured belt and a central citadel. With her masts and yards removed during a lengthy refit from 1890–97, she remained listed as a fighting unit until 1904, though with her obsolete muzzle-loading guns she could scarcely have been regarded as effective.

By contrast, the career of her contemporary *Captain* was tragically short. Designed to displace some 7,000 tons, she turned out to be very much overweight and so her already low freeboard was reduced even further. Only months after she joined the fleet in 1870, she capsized and sank in a squall in the Bay of Biscay, taking her designer, Cowper Coles, and most of her crew with her. The sailing rig was to continue in use in the next decade, but to many critics it was both hazardous and outdated.

Chapter Two

The Age of Experiment: 1870–1890

Despite the innovations embodied in *Warrior* and her successors, the armoured battleship in 1870 remained a vessel dependent in part on sails and largely restricted to broadside firing. But the breastwork monitors *Cerberus*, *Magdala* and *Abyssinia*, completed in that year, dispensed with sails altogether and each mounted four 10-inch guns, disposed in centre-line turrets. Together with the single turret *Glatton*, they pointed the way to the sea-going mastless ship.

Devastation and *Thunderer* carried this trend to its logical conclusion and were the first of their type. Displacing 9,300 tons and with low freeboard, each mounted four 35-ton guns in two turrets. When

HMS *Devastation*.

Devastation joined the fleet in 1873 she aroused great controversy. To the advocates of sail the squat, unlovely ship was a monstrosity, while her supporters waxed lyrical over her craggy virtues – she was 'an impregnable piece of Vauban fortification, with bastions, mounted upon a fighting coal mine'. Her full load of 1,800 tons of coal gave her a cruising radius of 4,700 miles and she had 2,500 tons of armour. Rearmed in 1891 with four 10-inch breech-loaders, the two ships served until 1907 by which time *Dreadnought*, which they had foreshadowed, had been commissioned.

An earlier *Dreadnought*, the fifth of her name, was completed in 1879 as a development of the *Devastation* design with a displacement larger by 1,500 tons, 38-ton guns and even heavier armour. She was the ultimate in the breastwork monitor, four smaller versions of which (the Cyclops class) had also been built. There was to be no clear line of development to the later *Dreadnought*; for the rest of the decade there was to be a return to the sailing rig. The French central battery ship *Redoutable* had a full rig of sails, while her half-sister *Alexandre* had a barque rig, with fore-and-aft sails on the mizzen mast. *Temeraire* had a massive two-masted brig rig and mounted her four 11-inch guns in barbettes fore and aft.

The ultimate in the masted battleship came in 1881 with *Inflexible*. She had the heaviest armour ever given to a warship before or since – 24-inch at its thickest – protecting a central citadel in which were mounted two circular turrets, each with two 16-inch guns. She was originally brig-rigged with two immense masts, though it was never intended that she would fight under sail, and when rebuilt in 1882 the sailing rig was removed.

She had been laid down as a reply to the Italian *Dandolo* and *Duilio* and was followed into service by two scaled-down versions, *Ajax* and *Agamemnon*. These, the last battleships in the Royal Navy to be armed with muzzle-loaders, have been described (by naval historian Oscar Parkes) as 'two of the most unsatisfactory ships ever built' for

HMS *Inflexible* (as rebuilt) in 1881.

the Royal Navy, and the next three acquisitions were little better. Two coastal defence ships, then building in a British yard for Turkey, were purchased and renamed *Belleisle* and *Orion*, and the third was the last broadside monitor *Superb*. Also purchased was *Independencia*, building at Millwall for the Brazilian Navy. Renamed *Neptune*, she was a mastless turret ship, resembling *Monarch* of a decade earlier.

The squadron, which was dispatched to Alexandria in 1882, epitomised the Royal Navy at this uncertain stage of its development. For the only major naval operation since the Crimean War, the ships were an ill-assorted group. The fleet comprised two turret ships – the new *Inflexible* and the old *Monarch*, four central battery ships – *Alexandra, Sultan, Superb* and *Invincible*, and the hybrid *Temeraire*. None of the three major mastless ships was present.

The French, who had at first intended to co-operate with Britain in suppressing the revolt against Ottoman rule by Arabi Pasha, did not do so and, with Egypt effectively passing under Britain's protection, rivalry between the two countries became intense. Consequently, the developments in French naval construction were watched even more closely. Since 1870 the French had built ten rigged central battery ships, of which the most recent and most powerful were *Redoutable, Courbet* and *Devastation*. Still building was *Admiral Duperre* with four 13.4-inch guns in barbettes, two on the centre line aft of the bridge and funnel, and one on either beam forward. The Italian naval architect Benedetto Brin designed the barbette ship *Italia* with four 17-inch guns in barbettes mounted diagonally amidships. She and her sister *Lepanto* achieved 18 knots and each had only a single pole mast amidships.

The Royal Navy had by now abandoned the muzzle-loader after the accident aboard *Thunderer* in 1879, and *Colossus* and *Edinburgh*, laid down in that year, were each equipped with four 12-inch breech loaders; earlier ships were converted during refits. Similarly *Inflexible*'s yards had been removed, leaving her with pole masts carrying fighting tops and a signal yard, similar modifications were carried out on earlier vessels. This left only *Swiftsure* and *Triumph* (on the China station) and the training ships *Northumberland, Minotaur* and *Agincourt* with a full sailing rig. The advantages of barbette mounting were recognised, though the much heavier turret was preferred in the ungainly *Conqueror* and *Hero*, which proved to have very poor sailing qualities, and finally in *Victoria* and *Sans Pareil*. However, *Collingwood* (9,500 tons), laid down in 1880, mounted her four 12-inch guns in open barbettes 20 feet above the waterline. Four more ships, *Anson, Camperdown, Howe* and *Rodney* each carried four 13.5-inch guns on a displacement of 10,000 tons, while *Benbow* mounted two 16.25-inch. With a heavy armoured belt and a top speed of 17 knots, they were considered to be a match for the latest French vessels of 1881 – *Hoche, Magenta, Marceau* and *Neptune*.

The decision to equip *Benbow* with the heaviest gun available had an unfortunate sequel. After the building of six ships of a basically similar design had given hopes of a more homogeneous battle fleet, there was now another change of heart. It was decided in 1885 that the next two ships, *Victoria* and *Sans Pareil*, should mount the giant 110 ton 16.25-inch guns in a single paired turret forward. They proved far from satisfactory and *Victoria* was only three years old when she was rammed and sunk by *Camperdown* during manoeuvres in the Gulf of Sirte. Nevertheless, the turret mounting was again chosen for *Nile* and *Trafalgar* in 1886. They were the last of the citadel turret ships.

The menace of the torpedo caused doubts to be cast on the future of the battleship in the 1880s. The 'Jeune Ecole' of French naval theorists contended that the building of smaller craft would enable a successful *guerre de course* (commerce raiding) and that this policy would be more rational than attempting to match Britain's battleship strength. By the end of the decade the Royal Navy had a massive superiority in numbers of capital ships, though the figure included too many outdated or inferior vessels to be entirely convincing. Nevertheless, in 1889 Britain

HMS Royal *Sovereign*.

had as many first class battleships as France and Russia combined and twice as many of the second class. A shortage of cruisers meant that the vital trade routes were vulnerable, and the Naval Defence Act of 1889 provided funding for seventy new ships over the next five years, of which forty-two were to be cruisers and ten battleships.

Since 1886 there had been a new Board of Admiralty, with a new Director of Naval Construction, W.H. White. The oldest ships still in service, including *Warrior* and *Black Prince*, as well as *Hector, Valiant* and *Defence* were now placed in reserve, and gunnery tests were carried out using the old *Resistance* as a target vessel. The result was the design for the Royal Sovereign class of seven ships, which marked

Battleship HMS *Royal Sovereign*, 1891. (© *National Maritime Museum, Greenwich, London*)

the beginning of a new era. They were to displace 14,150 tons and to have a cruising speed of 15 knots. The main armament comprised four 13.5-inch breech-loaders, mounted in pairs in two barbettes forward and aft of the superstructure, with a secondary armament of ten of the 6-inch quick-firing guns now regarded as essential for defence against torpedo attack. With a water-line armour belt and an underwater armoured deck, these ships set a new standard for battleship design for the next

HMS *Resolution*. (© *National Maritime Museum, Greenwich, London*)

decade. Oscar Parkes (a severe critic of many of the unsuitable designs of the past years) commented: 'For the first time since the *Devastation* set a new standard for unsightliness, a British battleship presented a proud, pleasing and symmetrical profile, initiating a new era of volcanic beauty after two decades of sullen and misshapen misfits.'

An eighth ship *Hood* was completed to a similar design, but with turrets instead of barbette mountings. Her lower freeboard, resulting from the great weight of the turrets, made her much inferior to her half-sisters, and she was the last turret ship to be built.

In the second class battleships *Barfleur* and *Centurion*, built at the same time and intended for the China station, the addition of protective hoods over the barbettes introduced the turret in its modern form, and the innovation was to be adopted as a standard feature in all subsequent ships of the Royal Navy. Together with the later and slightly larger *Renown*, these were the last second class battleships laid down for the Royal Navy. Two more, for Chile, were bought in 1904, when it was feared that they might be acquired by Russia.

The ships built under the 1889 Act all served with the fleet until the advent of dreadnoughts rendered them obsolete and they were taken out of service in the years immediately preceding the First World War. By then a new class of super-dreadnoughts was building and the names *Royal Sovereign, Royal Oak, Ramillies, Resolution* and *Revenge* together with *Renown* and *Repulse*, were earmarked for them.

Chapter Three

The Two Power Standard

The Royal Sovereigns were commissioned into the Navy during the years 1892–4, when a political rapprochement between France and Russia was developing towards ultimate alliance. This bond, at first derided by political cartoonists in England as the union of Beauty and the Beast (Marianne and the Russian bear), had serious repercussions, not least for naval policy. France's building programme of 1891 matched that of Britain by planning for ten new battleships and forty-five cruisers and caused considerable alarm. Although currently the Royal Navy had a margin of two battleships over the combined fleets of her two potential adversaries, a forecast showed that by 1898 this would have become a twenty-two to twenty-nine deficit. It was therefore decided that, as a matter of urgency, at least seven and preferably ten new battleships should be laid down in the years 1894–5.

Nine Majestics were built, to form with the Royal Sovereigns a homogeneous main battle fleet. Slightly larger than their immediate predecessors, the Majestics had a similar speed and the main armament of four 12-inch guns in two hooded barbettes, which was to be the standard for the remaining pre-dreadnoughts. Improved armour and an endurance of 7,600 miles at cruising speed made these the best-balanced capital ships of their time, and all were still in service in 1914. At this stage, French battleships had a higher freeboard and huge funnels and masts, to give them the appearance known as 'fierce-face', which made them seem antiquated by comparison with their British counterparts. An exaggerated tumble-home in the five ships *Charles*

Martel, Carnot, Jauréguiberry, Masséna and *Bouvet* enabled end-on fire from the 10.8-inch guns mounted as secondary armament on the beam, as well as the two 12-inch in single mountings fore and aft. The three ships of the Charlemagne class, with the larger *Iéna* and *Suffren*, each mounted four 12-inch in paired turrets, but the tumble-home was not reduced.

The Russians built in a similar style, beginning with the three ships of the Petropavlovsk class, armed with turrets of the French type, and continuing through to the Borodinos. Russian ambitions in Manchuria, and her leading part in the Dreibund (triple alliance of Germany, Austria-Hungary and Italy), which compelled Japan to surrender part of her territorial gains in the Sino-Japanese war, pushed Japan towards Britain. She had already ordered, in 1893, two ships of the Royal Sovereign type (*Fuji* and *Yashima*), to counter two German-built ships in the Chinese navy, and then four Majestics, enabling the overwhelming victory in the Russo-Japanese war of 1904–5. At Port Arthur, five Russian battleships, sunk or scuttled, were raised, refitted and served with the Japanese navy, while at the Battle of Tsushima Admiral Togo's four battleships sank three old and three new Russian battleships and captured *Orel* which then saw service as *Iwami*. Britain not only built ships and trained key personnel for Japan, but in 1902 had signed a treaty of alliance. This enabled her to bring home ships from the Pacific, but also to keep in home waters the new Canopus class, originally intended for the China station.

Canopus and her five sisters were laid down between December 1986 and August 1898, all entering service by 1902. Displacing 2,000 tons less than the Majestics, they carried the same armament and were slightly faster. The three Irresistibles were improved versions of the Canopus class and were followed into service by the five ships of the London class, completed in 1904. By the time they had entered service the Fashoda Crisis in East Africa had been followed first by the Anglo-French colonial agreement and then by the diplomatic moves

HMS *Canopus*.

H.M.S. Canopus, the British battleship which fired the first shot in the battle of the Falkland Islands.

which led to the Entente of 1904. With this rapprochement, France ceased to be a potential enemy, and the later French battleships of the Republique and Vérité classes were to be allies.

The new United States navy commissioned its first modern battleships in the 1880s, with the three Indianas mounting 13-inch guns and the similar *Iowa* with 12-inch guns. Eight more had been laid down by 1900, but these were not regarded as likely opponents for the Royal Navy. Their first action came in 1898, when *Maine* (recently reclassed as a second-class battleship instead of an armoured cruiser) blew up in the harbour at Havana. The accident was claimed to be sabotage and led to the brief Spanish–American War in which a US battle squadron blockaded Havana. Following a successful cruiser action at Manila Bay, the acquisition of the Philippines and Guam meant that the USA would now need a two-ocean navy and access across the Isthmus of Panama. The diplomatic activity necessary to create both the independent republic of Panama and the Canal Zone became a major preoccupation for the USA; the Canal itself was opened in 1914.

Nearer home, however, another new naval power was emerging. Since the creation of the German Empire in 1871, its navy had been

USS *Indiana*.

a very insignificant force, with the Siegfried class of eight coastal
defence vessels backed by cruisers and torpedo boats. The four
Brandenburgs were the first true German battleships armed with six
11-inch guns and they were followed by the four Kaisers with only
9.4-inch main armament. A new emphasis on naval building came with
the appointment of Grand Admiral Alfred von Tirpitz as Minister of
Marine in 1897.

Pressure from the German Navy League for an Imperial Navy to
match the strength of the army, and from the ambitions of the Kaiser,
led to the Navy Law of 1898. This envisaged a battle fleet of nineteen
ships by 1903 and entailed the building of ten new ships of the
Wittelsbach and Braunschweig classes to add to the ships in service.

These retained the lighter armament of their predecessors (9.4-inch and 11-inch respectively), and they proved to be of little fighting value when war came. Along with the two remaining Brandenburgs (whose two sisters had been sold to Turkey in 1910), they were all employed on harbour duties and most were ultimately disarmed. *Zahringen* was converted into a radio-controlled target vessel in 1926, but three of the Braunschweigs were retained as coastal defence ships in the 1920s, the other two serving as unarmed depot ships.

Grand Admiral Alfred von Tirpitz.

SMS *Braunschweig*.

A second Navy Law in 1900 revised the programme, establishing a new target for a battle fleet of thirty-eight ships by 1920. These would comprise four squadrons of eight ships, with four in reserve and two fleet flagships, which would give the German nation a fleet little inferior to that of Britain. It was apparent that the ships had a short range with cramped crew quarters, the ships' companies, when in harbour, living in barracks ashore. They were clearly designed for operations in the North Sea. Tirpitz had evolved a 'risk' strategy, creating a fleet so strong that Britain could not afford to chance the loss of her naval supremacy by the damage which a clash of the two fleets would entail. This, he reasoned, would give Germany massive diplomatic bargaining power.

HMS *King Edward VII*.

There had been little concern in Britain over the initial German plan: in 1898 the Royal Navy had the sixteen ships of the Royal Sovereign and Majestic classes already built, six of the Canopus class building, and eight more of the Formidable and London classes planned – all vessels superior in every way to the German ships. Britain's advantages in design experience and in dockyard capacity should, it was felt, keep her well ahead. The 1899 programme envisaged the six Duncans,

Battleship HMS *Dominion* at anchor at Spithead. (© *National Maritime Museum, Greenwich, London*)

designed to be a match for the latest Russian ships, and mounting four
12-inch and twelve 6-inch guns. Further additions to the fleet were
the two second class battleships building at Barrow and at Elswick for
the Chilean Navy. The 10-inch *Libertad* and *Constitucion* were bought
and renamed *Triumph* and *Swiftsure*. Like their earlier namesakes, they
were originally destined for the China station, but were sent to the
Dardanelles in 1915.

The first direct response to the German building programme,
outlined in the second Navy Law, was the King Edward VII class.
These eight vessels, each of 16,350 tons, were larger than any earlier
ships and mounted, in addition to a main armament of four 12-inch
guns, a secondary battery of four 9.2-inch in single turrets on the upper
deck. In 1912 *Africa* was used for an early experiment in naval aviation
when the first take-off from a ship was achieved from a platform built
over one of her turrets, while later in the year a similar venture aboard
Hibernia saw the first take-off from a ship under way.

The last two pre-dreadnoughts built for the Royal Navy were laid
down in 1905 and continued the innovation of a secondary battery of
9.2-inch guns – no fewer than ten of them, all mounted in upper deck

HMS *Agamemnon*.

Battleship HMS *Agamemnon* at anchor at Spithead, with awning rigged aft and *Lord Nelson* astern of her. (© *National Maritime Museum, Greenwich, London*)

turrets, to the complete exclusion of the 6-inch battery. Construction of *Lord Nelson* and *Agamemnon* was delayed by the priority given to *Dreadnought* (even their 12-inch main armament being diverted) and they did not enter service until 1908. They were considerably more powerful than the ships building in Germany at the same time: the five Deutschlands were still armed with 11-inch guns.

The French had laid down, between 1901 and 1903, two Républiques and four Vérités, abandoning some of the more exaggerated features of their older ships, but still taking so long to build that they were almost obsolete before they entered service. Of these *Liberté* blew up at Toulon in 1911. The next class, the six Dantons were similar to

Russian pre-dreadnought *Kniaz Potemkin.*

the Lord Nelsons in that they each had a secondary battery of twelve 9.4-inch guns, but they were not in service until 1911.

The Russian navy had suffered grievously in the war with Japan, from which she emerged with seven elderly battleships, of dubious value even as coastal defence vessels. Only two ships, *Potemkin* and *Tsesarevitch* had been completed since 1900 and both owed much to French influence in their design. *Potemkin* was part of the Black Sea fleet, gaining her niche in history when her crew mutinied in Odessa in 1905; she subsequently relived that event when she was the setting for Eisenstein's film 'Battleship Potemkin' celebrating the heroism of the mutineers.

To these was added the *Slava*, last of the Borodinos, fortunate to have been completed a month after Tsushima. Only four more pre-dreadnoughts were built: two of the Evstafi class and two Imperator Pavels which joined the Black Sea and Baltic fleets in 1910.

The prizes taken by the Japanese at Port Arthur and Tsushima proved of limited use as fighting ships. Two saw service as coastal defence ships, three as guard ships and two as training vessels: only the *Retvisan* saw active service under her new name of *Hizen*. The last two battleships built in British yards for Japan were the *Kashima* and *Katori*, similar to the King Edwards, but with a secondary battery of 10-inch guns. Four smaller ships were built in Japan by 1909, while the *Aki* and *Satsuma* were laid down in 1905. Intended originally for an all-big-gun armament, they were completed as 'intermediate dreadnoughts' of the Lord Nelson type, with four 12-inch and twelve 10-inch guns.

Italy and Austria-Hungary, though members of the Triple Alliance with Germany, were rivals for territory in the Tyrol and Istria and their naval strength was built up with a keen regard for one another. Italy, for whom Benedetto Brin had been a resourceful and original designer, had lagged so far in naval construction that in 1900 she possessed only four obsolete battleships as guard-ships with two more as disarmed depot vessels. Two 10-inch gunned ships of only 9,800 tons were ready by 1902, and were based in Venice, while the larger *Benedetto Brin* and *Regina Margherita* took station at Brindisi. Four ships of the Regina Elena class of 12,750 tons and armed with only two 12-inch and twelve 8-inch guns were ready by 1908 and were based at Taranto. To counter this fleet the Austrians too had a collection of old ships, and a succession of very small battleships mounting no more than 9.4-inch guns. The three of the Wien class were appropriately rated as coastal defence ships, but the Habsburgs were seen as sea-going battleships, despite their meagre 8,340 tons and three 9.4-inch guns. The three Erzherzog Karls were only a marginal improvement, and it was not until 1911 that the Austrians possessed three full-size ships, the Radetzky class of 14,500 tons and with four 12-inch and eight 9.4-inch, comparable with the King Edwards of a decade earlier.

Not only the major powers were intent on deploying battleships. The South American republics followed suit, placing orders in European and American yards, while Greece and Turkey, as ever eying one another nervously, each purchased two old vessels from America and Germany respectively. The Scandinavian countries and the Netherlands were content with coastal defence ships.

The American navy, however, continued to grow. Twelve modern battleships were in service by 1904, by which time the turrets and 13-inch guns of the earlier vessels had given way to hooded barbettes and 12-inch guns in the more recent. The five Virginias of the 1902 programme (all in service by 1906) were comparable with their contemporaries in the Royal Navy in that they each displaced 15,000 tons and were armed with four 12-inch and twelve 6-inch guns. They differed in that they mounted four of their secondary battery of eight 8-inch guns in paired turrets, on top of the 12-inch main armament. This was intended to give a better field of fire, but in practice problems caused by blast made the system unworkable and it was not attempted again. The six Connecticut class of the 1903 programme were of a more conventional layout, with all the 8-inch guns in paired turrets on the beam. They were followed by the smaller and slower *Mississippi* and *Idaho* which later were sold to Greece and renamed *Lemnos* and *Kilkis*. By the time of their completion in 1908, however, the design for the South Carolinas had triggered a new era in battleship construction.

Chapter Four

The Age of the Dreadnought 1906–1908

The last battleships of the pre-dreadnought era embodied technical improvement both in defence and hitting power. The use of nickel steel made for a reduction in the thickness of the armour belt, and to the extension of the area which could be protected on a given tonnage, while the curved armoured deck, double bottom and anti-torpedo bulkheads gave added protection against the new dangers of the mine and the torpedo. More efficient propellants and breech mechanisms improved the main armament and enabled action at longer range outside the menace of the torpedo boats, the quick-firing 6-inch gun being developed as defence against such vessels.

The consequent changes in gunnery theory in turn had a profound impact on ship design. Ranging by firing salvoes was more efficient, but the increasing calibre of the secondary armament began to cause problems. The 9.2-inch guns of the King Edwards had a different trajectory and flight time for a given range than the 12-inch of the main battery, but the shell splashes were not identifiably different, with consequent problems in gunnery control. The clear answer was the elimination of the intermediate battery and the reliance upon heavy guns of a single calibre: the outcome was the building of *Dreadnought*.

A larger main battery was not in itself an innovation. The Russian battleships of the Ekaterina II class had mounted six 12-inch, in a curious triangular disposition. One of the three barbettes, with a pair of 12-inch guns, was on the centre line aft, while the others were mounted forward on each beam. A decade later the Brandenburgs mounted six 11-inch in three centreline turrets. Then, in 1903, the Italian Vittorio Cuniberti had outlined in *Jane's Fighting Ships* a new battleship for the Royal Navy. This was to displace 17,000 tons, to be capable of 24 knots and to carry twelve 12-inch guns in four double and four single turrets. With two turrets on the centre line, eight guns could fire on either broadside and four ahead or astern.

Admiral Sir John ('Jackie') Fisher.

At the time the Royal Navy enjoyed a massive superiority over any foreseeable combination of adversaries: in addition to the eight King Edwards and the two Lord Nelsons planned, there were thirty-six battleships of modern design in commission. These, from the Royal Sovereigns to the Duncans, would be so far outclassed by Cuniberti's ship as to be of limited use, and it was an opinion widely held that Britain should not initiate a change which would eliminate the advantage built up so carefully and expensively over the years.

The appointment of Sir John Fisher as First Sea Lord in 1904 ensured a whole series of reforms in the training of personnel, the disposition of the fleet, and the organisation of an effective reserve.

It also ensured that *Dreadnought* would be built. The assumption henceforth was that Germany was the potential enemy and the battle fleets were to be deployed accordingly. Previously, the most modern battleships had been assigned to the Mediterranean Fleet; a dozen of the best ships served there, with older ships in smaller numbers in the Channel and Home Fleets, or on detached service further afield. The alliance of 1902 with Japan and the Entente of 1904 with France enabled Fisher to alter the entire pattern. By leaving the Pacific largely to Japan and the Mediterranean to France, he could base an enlarged

HMS *Black Prince*, 1914.

Home Fleet of sixteen battleships on Dover and an Atlantic Fleet of eight more at Gibraltar. This enabled the bulk of the battle fleet to be deployed against Germany.

Fisher next turned his attention to the disposal of elderly ships, still on the reserve list, but of no real fighting value. These included almost forty old battleships, stretching back to *Warrior* and *Black Prince*, now rated as armoured cruisers. Others were training or depot ships, but progressively over the next few years all those built before 1885 went to the scrap-yards.

Fisher was not only an advocate of the all-big-gun battleship, but was also aware that the concept was being regarded with some interest by other navies. By 1904, the Japanese were considering the design of a ship of 17,000 tons, armed with eight 12-inch guns, and by the time the two Satsumas were laid down early in 1905, the armament had been

increased to twelve 12-inch. Also, in 1905, the new naval programme
authorised by the United States Congress approved the building of
two South Carolinas mounting eight 12-inch. To Fisher, therefore, the
arguments against Britain initiating naval change were unconvincing:
that change was already beginning, and it was to Britain's advantage to
seize an early lead.

From a series of six draft designs, offering different combinations
of engines and armament, the plans for *Dreadnought* were chosen, and
she was given priority even to the extent of using materials already
acquired for the building of other ships – including the four 12-inch
turrets and a spare, intended for *Lord Nelson* and *Agamemnon*. Her keel
was laid down at Portsmouth on 2 October 1905, she was launched in
February 1906 and commissioned on 3 October 1906. Of 17,900 tons,
she mounted ten 12-inch guns in five turrets, three on the centre line
and two on the beam, to give a broadside of eight guns, with six able
to fire forward. Turbines gave her a speed of 21 knots, but their greater
reliability gave her a cruising speed equal to the top speed of earlier
ships. Moreover, she was able to hold her speed for hours, whereas
reciprocating, or piston engines grew progressively less efficient.

HMS *Dreadnought*.

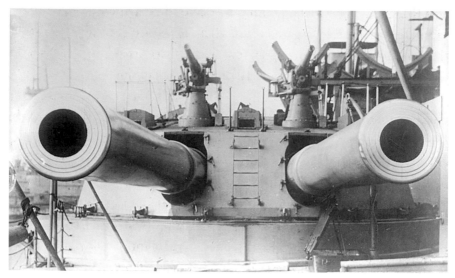

12-inch gun turret aboard *Dreadnought*.

Although the battleship programmes of Japan and the United States had helped precipitate the Admiralty into building *Dreadnought*, both of these two countries were on good terms with Britain, and there was no real possibility of a war involving them. France and Russia had been the likeliest adversaries, but since 1898, relations with both of these countries had improved, and it was now Germany on whom suspicious eyes were cast. Political hostility concerning events in South Africa, South America and Morocco was intensified by the German Navy Laws and by the Kaiser's assumption of the title of 'Admiral of the Atlantic' in 1902. Whether this was simply a piece of flamboyance, or whether it had any serious intent, is impossible to assess, but there was no way to ignore the physical presence of the new German battle fleet. Fifteen battleships had been laid down between 1899 and 1905 and these seemed to be a direct threat to Britain's naval supremacy. This convinced the Admiralty that 'the German fleet has been designed for a possible conflict with the British fleet. It cannot be designed for the purpose of playing a leading part in any future war with France and Russia, a war which can only be decided by armies and on land'. Germany, it was felt, was not dependent upon ocean trade routes and the need to maintain a margin of superiority over that country became the overriding consideration in British naval planning.

It was to give Britain a lead in the new naval race that *Dreadnought* had been laid down and completed with such urgency. This had an immediate effect abroad, where naval building plans were halted and amended to take account of the new vessel. The Japanese *Satsuma* and *Aki*, laid down in 1905, were not completed until 1909 and 1911 respectively, and then were revealed to be 'intermediate dreadnoughts' of the same type as the Lord Nelsons. Eight of the planned 12-inch guns were replaced by 10-inch, with only four 12-inch left as the main armament, a change dictated by economic rather than naval requirements. The American South Carolinas, authorised in 1905, were not laid down until 1906 nor were they completed until 1908. They did, however, incorporate one significant design advantage in their four centreline turrets, in two pairs fore and aft, with the second and third mounted higher than the first and fourth. This device of 'super-firing' turrets was not introduced into the Royal Navy until 1909, nor was there a British battleship with a complete centreline armament until 1912. Russia and France did not even begin to build dreadnoughts until 1909 and 1910 respectively, while Italy and Japan also laid down their first in 1909. Germany's first dreadnoughts were the four Nassaus, begun in 1907, but these were armed only with 11-inch guns, and the first of them did not enter service until 1909.

By then it had been possible in Britain to capitalise on the advantage of the initiative gained by building *Dreadnought*. Three more great ships had been laid down under the 1905 6 programme and completed in 1908, and three more were begun in each of the 1906–7 and 1907–8 programmes. Yet another four had been laid down before *Nassau* was commissioned. It appeared that not only the first round, but also the second and third, had gone to Britain, but Germany did not give up, and the naval race was under way.

The three Invincibles, laid down in 1906 and completed two years later, represented another new design concept. In addition to the Dreadnought project, which he had designated HMS 'Untakeable', Fisher had been a keen advocate of a fast vessel which he called HMS 'Unapproachable'. This was to enter service as the battle cruiser, a design which caused yet more controversy. The function of this ship was essentially that of the armoured cruiser, but it was to have the same margin of superiority in speed, armament and range, over existing armoured cruisers as did *Dreadnought* over earlier battleships. They were to be 'super-scouting cruisers' able to press home their reconnaissance of an enemy fleet in the face of hostile armoured cruisers, and were to be fast enough to hunt down commerce raiders. But it was the calibre of their main armament – 12-inch guns in the earlier classes – which led to their being designated 'dreadnoughts'. This marked them down

HMS *Invincible*.

HMS *Invincible* anchored at Spithead.

for a third function in which they were to prove highly vulnerable – as a fast wing to the battlefleet. Three, including *Inflexible* herself, were to be lost in action at Jutland, proving their unsuitability for this role. However, in 1908 when *Inflexible, Invincible* and *Indomitable* joined the fleet, they were hailed as welcome innovations, despite the doubts of the more perceptive. In 1906, when they were still building, Brassey wrote: 'Vessels of this enormous size and cost are unsuitable for many of the duties of cruisers, but an even stronger objection is that an admiral, having Invincibles in his fleet, will be certain to put them in the line of battle, where their comparatively light protection would be a disadvantage, and their high speed of no value.'

HMS *Inflexible*.

A decade before Jutland, he drew attention to the danger of their
magazines being penetrated by plunging fire at long range.

Dreadnought herself was less well protected than her near-
contemporaries, the Lord Nelsons, and her main armament was
not disposed to the best advantage. Her fore-funnel was placed
immediately abaft the bridge, with the signal mast beyond it, an
inconvenient arrangement corrected in the Bellerophons. By the time
of the outbreak of war in 1914, she had been so much eclipsed by later
developments that she no longer formed part of the Grand Fleet but
instead was flagship of the Channel Fleet, composed otherwise of the
pre-dreadnoughts of the King Edward VII class, and at the end of the
war was sold for scrap. Yet she, like *Warrior* and *Devastation* before her,
had ushered in a new era of naval design.

Chapter Five

The Naval Race 1908–1914

ermany's programme of battleship construction, which
had begun so well in the years following the passage of the
two Navy Laws, received a severe set-back with the news
of the building of *Dreadnought*. Consideration had been given to the
building of such a vessel in Germany, but the ships under construction
in 1906 were far inferior. The *Deutschland* was completed in July of
that year, but her four sisters were not in service until 1907 and 1908.
A projected design with twelve heavy guns, of two different calibres,
similar to Britain's Lord Nelsons, but of smaller size and with lesser-
calibre guns, had been abandoned in favour of a design with eight
11-inch on 17,000 tons displacement. By 1906, with information
available about *Dreadnought*, this was again modified so that twelve
11-inch guns were mounted in the Nassaus. These were disposed
with four of the six turrets mounted on the beam, so that even with
two guns more than *Dreadnought*, they still had only an eight gun

SMS *Nassau*.

broadside of 5,280 pounds against 6,800. With reciprocating engines rather than turbines, and capable of only 19 knots, they were clearly inferior to *Dreadnought* in all respects save two. In weight of armour and in internal subdivision into watertight compartments, the Nassaus were much superior to the prototype; Germany maintained these advantages in all the first-generation dreadnoughts of the pre-war era.

Nassau and her sisters *Westfalen, Rheinland* and *Posen* did not join the fleet until 1909–10. By then the Royal Navy had built not only the three Invincible class battle cruisers, but also three Bellerephons. These were basically enlarged versions of *Dreadnought*, at 18,600 tons, and with sixteen 4-inch guns as anti-torpedo-boat weapons. They retained the wing turret mounting for four of the main calibre guns, although super-firing turrets were incorporated into *Minas Gerais* and *São Paolo*, built in British yards between 1907–10 for the Brazilian navy. *Collingwood, St Vincent* and *Vanguard*, laid down under the 1907 programme and completed by 1910, were again broadly similar and

SMS *Von der Tann*.

gave the Royal Navy seven dreadnought battleships and three battle cruisers to the four and one of Germany.

Von der Tann, Germany's first battle cruiser, was laid down as part of yet another revised programme of naval building by Germany. A new Navy Law in 1907 proposed the building of three dreadnought battleships and one battle cruiser each year for the next four years, with two each year thereafter until 1918, to give a total of twenty-eight by 1918. This coincided with a cutback in naval building in Britain by the Liberal government which had taken office in 1906. Impressed by the lead in ships completed and building and anxious to reduce the expenditure upon defence, it determined that only two battleships need be built each year. For 1907–8 indeed, there were originally plans only for two St Vincents, but the failure of disarmament talks at The Hague led to an increase to three. The 1908–9 programme provided only for a single battleship, *Neptune*, and one battle cruiser, *Indefatigable*. In each of these, the wing turrets were offset to allow a limited arc of cross-deck fire, enabling the full broadside to be employed. Considerations of blast damage meant that these turrets could not be used for end-on fire, a limitation which applied also to

SMS *Helgoland*.

Battleship HMS *Superb* at anchor at Spithead. (© *National Maritime Museum, Greenwich, London*)

the superimposed rear turrets of *Neptune*. In reply, the Germans were building the first three Helgolands, enlarged versions of the Nassaus, and the battle cruiser *Moltke*. For the latter they retained the 11-inch gun, but the battleships were armed with 12-inch, still mounted in hexagon formation with four beam turrets.

Gloomy forecasts of the erosion, not only of the two-power standard, but also of Britain's naval superiority over Germany, now began to be heard. Various calculations suggested that Germany might achieve a lead by 1914 at the latest, and the government in London was put under heavy pressure to increase its 1909–10 programme. In 1908, when the first moves were made, the Admiralty asked for four dreadnoughts to be authorised for the next year, with a provision for an increase to six if necessary. In this they had the support of Sir Edward Grey, the Foreign Secretary, but were opposed both by Lloyd George, as Chancellor of the Exchequer, and by Winston Churchill, President of the Board of Trade, both of whom insisted that four would be enough.

Despite a campaign by elements of the press and by the Navy League for eight, the Admiralty rested on its calculations. At that point, of the seven battleships and two battle cruisers laid down by Germany, none was complete. Moreover the widening of the Kiel Canal, vital to allow

HMS *Hercules*.

HMS *Hercules* at Scapa Flow.

the easy passage from the bases and exercise areas of the Baltic, was at an early stage and Germany's North Sea defences were inadequate. Nevertheless, the fear that a crisis might draw away some of the battle fleet persisted, and was given more immediacy by the Bosnian annexation dispute between Austria-Hungary and Russia, and by the Casablanca incident involving Germany and France, both of which occurred in 1908.

By early 1909 Britain had seven dreadnoughts in commission, with five building. Though Germany as yet had none in service, she had ten building, to be ready by 1912, and with her plans to build four a year, she would soon be ahead of Britain. Fears began to grow, based on the calculation that Krupps had the capacity to arm eight dreadnoughts a year.

The newspaper cry went up 'We want eight, and we won't wait', with both *The Times* and the *Daily Telegraph* joining in the campaign.

HMS *Lion*.

An article in the *Observer* demanded 'the eight, the whole eight and nothing but the eight' and eventually the Cabinet offered a compromise. Four ships were to be included in the 1909–10 programme, with the provision for four more to be included by April 1910 'if it appeared necessary'. This was on the understanding that these would be additional ships 'without prejudice to the 1910–11 programme' rather

SMS *Goeben*.

than the anticipation of the next year's plans. The ships were all to be completed by 1912, so restoring the Royal Navy's precarious advantage. Churchill was to write of this decision: 'a curious and characteristic decision was reached. The Admiralty had demanded six ships, the Treasury offered four, and we eventually compromised on eight.'

Provided for in the 1909–10 Estimates were the two 20,000 ton half-sisters to *Neptune*, named *Colossus* and *Hercules*. These retained the unusual layout of the main armament which had characterised the earlier ship, but the four Orions showed two significant changes. They disposed all ten guns of the main armament in five centre-line turrets, in two super firing pairs fore and aft with one turret amidships. This layout meant an increase in displacement of 22,500 tons; moreover the guns were of 13.5-inch calibre, firing a shell of 1,250 pounds against the 850 of the 12-inch gun. The same calibre gun was mounted in the two ships of the eight gun battle cruisers which completed the programme. These were *Lion* and *Princess Royal*, of 26,500 tons and capable of 27 knots.

HMS *Indefatigable*.

To complete the advantage were two ships which did not feature in the British naval estimates at all. The battle cruisers *Australia* and *New Zealand*, sister ships to the *Indefatigable* were laid down in June 1910. On completion in 1912, *New Zealand* was placed at the disposal of the Admiralty. *Australia* was stationed in the Pacific at the outbreak of war, but joined the Grand Fleet in 1915.

Germany maintained her programme of four ships a year. In 1909–10 these included the fourth of the Helgolands, named *Oldenburg* and the battle cruiser *Goeben*. The others were *Kaiser* and *Friedrich der Grosse*, of 25,000 tons. Each mounted ten 12-inch guns in a pattern very similar to *Neptune*, with offset beam turrets. Three further ships of this class, together with the battle cruiser *Seydlitz*, followed in the 1910–11 programme. Britain countered these with the four King George Vs and the battle cruiser *Queen Mary*, all with 13.5-inch guns. All of these ships were complete by the end of 1913, to widen the gap in Britain's favour. She then had eighteen dreadnought battleships and nine battle cruisers (if we include *Australia* and *New Zealand*) against Germany's thirteen and four. This was not a two-power standard; by then the aim was for a margin of sixty per cent superiority over Germany.

Other countries were being discounted in the calculations. France was linked with Britain by the 1904 Entente and the 1913 Naval Agreement

Italian dreadnought *Dante Alighieri*.

arranged for a concentration of her naval strength in the Mediterranean. In 1912 France could deploy fourteen pre-dreadnoughts and the six 'semi-dreadnoughts' of the Danton class at Toulon and Oran to counter the eight old battleships of Italy and the nine of Austria-Hungary. Although these countries were both members, with Germany, of the Triple Alliance, disputes over the ownership of Italia Irredenta – the Tyrol, Trentino and Istria – meant that their naval building was directed at least as much against each other as against any foreign enemy. Moreover, mutual recognition of colonial claims in Libya and Morocco respectively had eased Franco-Italian relations, and Italy had always said that she would not engage in war with Britain.

All three countries had begun to build dreadnoughts, but progress was slow and the first ships were not ready until shortly before the outbreak of war. By August 1914, France has commissioned the four Courbets which had taken three years to build. Of 23,500 tons displacement, they were capable of only 20 knots; armed with twelve 12-inch guns, four of which were mounted in wing turrets, they were seriously weaker than any contemporary. Their successors, *Bretagne, Lorraine* and *Provence* were basically similar to the Orions with a centre-line armament and guns of 13.4-inch calibre. They too were somewhat under-armoured, and they did not enter service until 1915–16.

Italian dreadnought
Leonardo da Vinci.

HMS *Superb*, 1907, pictured shortly after completion.

Italy's first dreadnought, *Dante Alighieri*, was designed by Cuniberti, but showed significant alterations to his original design of 1903. The twelve guns of the main 12-inch battery were mounted in four triple turrets, all on the centre-line, and there was a secondary battery of twenty 4.7-inch, of which eight were in paired turrets abreast of A and D turrets. Like most Italian warships, before and since, she was capable of high speed, reaching 24 knots on her acceptance trials in 1913. A development of this design was seen in the three larger vessels of the Cavour class, laid down in 1910. The principle of centre-line armament and the triple turret were retained, but in place of the two turrets mounted amidships, the Cavours had only one. Two paired turrets were mounted to fire over the forward and aft turrets, to give

Japanese *Kongo* class battle-cruiser *Haruna* (as rebuilt).

USS *New York*.

HMS *Superb* anchored in the Thames Estury, 1909.

the unusual total of thirteen big guns in five turrets. The secondary armament was mounted in casemates at upper deck level, and again the ships were rather lacking in defensive armour to gain another knot or two in speed. *Giulio Cesare* was commissioned in 1914, *Conti di Cavour* and *Leonardo da Vinci* in 1915, but the latter was lost when she blew up at her moorings in harbour at Taranto in August 1916.

The first Austrian dreadnoughts were also to be the last. The four ships of the Tegetthoff class were designed in 1910 to carry twelve 12-inch on a displacement of 20,000 tons. With the main armament in four triple turrets, B and C mounted to fire over A and D, they were an economical and effective design. The first three were in service by 1914 and were based at Pola throughout the war, but *Szent István* was built in the Danubius yard at Fiume, a political decision to gain the support of the Hungarian delegates in the Assembly of the Dual Monarchy when the estimates were approved. She was the first battleship to be built there and took almost four years to complete.

Russia too adopted the triple turret for her dreadnoughts. Although none of the four Ganguts was ready at the outbreak of war, all were in service by December 1914. They had been authorised in 1907 and

HMS *Glatton* circa 1914.

HMS *Alexandra* at Malta. This painting, by a Maltese artist, shows the *Alexandra* flying the St George's flag at the main, a white ensign at the stern and a Union Jack on the end of her bowsprit. She has the battleship *Dreadnought* under her bow and the *Colossus* on her left. (BHC3183 © *National Maritime Museum, Greenwich, London*)

HMS *Trafalgar*. (BHC3672 © *National Maritime Museum, Greenwich, London*)

HMS *Colossus*, Captain Cyprian Bridge. (PU6285 © *National Maritime Museum, Greenwich, London*)

A painting showing HMS *Hope* being towed into Emsenanda de la Malata by HMS *Seahorse* with salvage steamers alongside, April 1893. Water can be seen pouring out of the ship as the careful operation gets under way and small boats hover round the ship. (BHC3410 © *National Maritime Museum, Greenwich, London*)

HMS *Camperdown* ramming HMS *Victoria* off Tripoli, 22 June 1893. (PU6305 © *National Maritime Museum, Greenwich, London*)

Painting of HMS *Canopus* launched at Portsmouth, 13 October 1897. (PU0289 © *National Maritime Museum, Greenwich, London*)

Painting of HMS *London* named and launched at Portsmouth, 21 September 1899. (PU6312 © *National Maritime Museum, Greenwich, London*)

FFred Mitchell
1907

2655

HMS *Dreadnought* no. 2655. (PU9489 © *National Maritime Museum, Greenwich, London*)

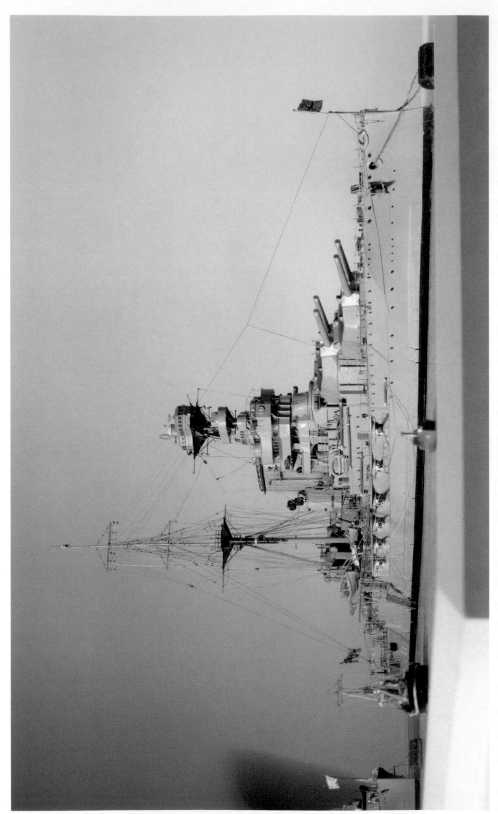

Scale model of the Dreadnought battleship, HMS *Queen Elizabeth*. (D9119-C © *National Maritime Museum, Greenwich, London*)

laid down in 1909, but their building had taken so long that they were virtually obsolescent by the time they were completed. They had two turrets amidships, restricting end-on fire to only three guns ahead or astern. They were assigned to the Baltic Fleet, and the succeeding *Imperatrica Maria*, *Imperator Aleksander III* and *Ekaterina II* to the Black Sea. They broadly resembled the earlier ships, but were two knots slower, while a fourth, to be known as *Imperator Nikolaj I* was to have mounted eight 16-inch guns, but was never completed.

Spain built three small dreadnoughts at Ferrol between 1909 and 1915, each of 15,700 tons and mounting eight 12-inch guns. The smallest dreadnoughts ever built, each was armed with eight 12-inch guns provided by Armstrongs and powered by turbines produced by Parsons. Greece was the only other European country to contemplate owning dreadnoughts, and *Salamis* was laid down at the Vulkan yard in Hamburg, but was never completed.

Battleship HMS *Temeraire* at anchor at Spithead. (© *National Maritime Museum, Greenwich, London*)

Japan and America were, of course, the other two naval powers of significance. By 1906 Japan was building her own warships, and *Aki* and *Satsuma*, though conceived as dreadnoughts, were actually completed with a mixed heavy armament. *Kawachi* and *Settsu*, with twelve 12-inch guns (of two different types), were commissioned in 1912 and the next two, *Fuso* and *Yamashiro* mounted twelve 14-inch in six twin turrets. Four early battle cruisers (*Tsukuba, Ikoma, Ibuki* and *Kurama*) were each armed with four 12-inch before the battle cruiser *Kongo* became the last Japanese vessel to be built in England, by Vickers at Barrow-in-Furness. Of 27,500 tons, she carried eight 14-inch guns and could raise 27.5 knots, and three sisters (*Hiei, Haruna* and *Kirishima*) were then built to the same design in Japanese yard.

The United States laid down two battleships each year from 1906, with increasing tonnage and calibre of guns, so that *New York* and *Texas*, which joined the Atlantic Fleet in 1914, mounted ten 14-inch guns on 27,000 tons.

She now had ten dreadnoughts in service, with four more building; all featured the lattice masts which were so distinctive of American-built ships. The USA was now clearly the world's third naval power, behind Britain and Germany, but ahead of the emergent Japan and well ahead of the declining naval strength of France or Russia.

With Japan as an ally, with France and Russia members of the 1907 Triple Entente, and with no likelihood of hostilities with the USA, it was only Germany which presented any threat to Britain. She had laid down three battleships of the König class, but was still arming her ships with 12-inch guns. Britain countered with the four Iron Dukes, and the battle cruiser *Tiger* (ten and eight 13.5-inch respectively. These were the last ships completed by the end of 1914 and Britain had more ships building than had Germany. The advantage in the naval race had gone very clearly to Britain.

Chapter Six

Dreadnoughts at War – 1914–1918

In August 1914 the Royal Navy had what seemed to be an unassailable lead in capital ships over Germany's High Seas Fleet. Already in service were twenty dreadnought battleships and nine battle cruisers, against fourteen and four. Building in British yards, and commissioned by December were the last two Iron Dukes and the battle cruiser *Tiger*.

In addition two ships being built for Turkey were completed in August of 1914. *Reshadieh*, built by Vickers at Barrow, with ten 13.5-inch guns on 22,780 tons was similar to *Iron Duke*. *Sultan Osman I* built by Armstrongs on the Tyne, laid down for Brazil as *Rio de Janeiro* but purchased by Turkey in 1912, had fourteen 12-inch in seven centre-line turrets. Both were taken into the Royal Navy as *Erin* and *Agincourt* respectively.

HMS *Iron Duke*.

HMS *Agincourt*.

The Chilean *Almirante Latorre* with ten 14-inch guns was in an advanced state of completion and was commissioned as HMS *Canada*, while her sister ship, *Almirante Cochrane*, was completed as the aircraft carrier HMS *Eagle*. Against these, Germany completed three König class and the battle cruiser *Derfflinger* by the end of the year. Although the latter was offset by the sale of *Goeben* to Turkey, she had been replaced by *Lutzow* by March 1916. Elsewhere the fleets of France and Russia were comparable in strength with those of Italy and Austria-Hungary. It was President Woodrow Wilson's avowed policy to keep the United States out of the war, but in the Pacific Japan was a valuable ally to Britain.

In the further building programme, Britain was in an even stronger position. In 1912 the decision had been taken to increase the size of the main armament to 15-inch for the ships of the Queen Elizabeth class. This gun fired a shell of 1,920 pounds against the 1,250 pounds of the 13.5-inch. The total weight of the guns, barbettes, turrets and magazine protection for four 15-inch twin turrets was virtually the same as for five 13.5-inch, for a broadside almost 3,000 pounds heavier.

Another innovation was the use of oil fuel which gave a forty per cent increase in radius of action for an equivalent fuel load. The Americans had already introduced oil fuel into the Nevada class, but there was hesitation in Britain over a step which would make her dependent on overseas resources when she had plentiful stocks of the best Welsh anthracite. The government purchase in 1914, of controlling shares in the Anglo-Persian Oil Company, at a cost of two million pounds was a natural sequel. The first three of the ships,

Admiral Sir John Jellicoe.

Queen Elizabeth, *Warspite* and *Barham* were completed by 1915, and *Valiant* and *Malaya* the following year.

A further class of 15-inch gunned ships was planned for the financial years 1913–14, and five were laid down before war began. These were the Revenge class, coal-burning and rather slower, at 23 knots. Four

HMS *Queen Elizabeth*.

Battleship HMS *Valiant* anchored in Alexandria harbour taking on ammunition. (© *National Maritime Museum, Greenwich, London*)

were in service by 1916 and the fifth in the following year. Two more, *Renown* and *Repulse* were completed as battle cruisers in 1916. They mounted six 15-inch guns and were capable of 32 knots, but spent so much time in dockyard hands that they were known in the fleet as HMS Refit and HMS Repair.

The concentration on the numbers of ships tended to mask other considerations. Britain had a further advantage in the calibre of guns. The Germans continued to use the 11-inch gun when the 12-inch was standard in the Royal Navy; by the time that they had adopted the 12-inch, Britain had moved to 13.5-inch and then to 15-inch. However, the poor quality of British shells led to the frustration of hits being observed without significant damage caused, and the unstable nature of cordite led to the loss of *Vanguard* by internal explosion in 1917. The ships of the High Seas Fleet were also much better protected, both by heavier armour and by internal subdivision, proving that they could absorb a great deal of punishment. After Jutland, the battered *Seydlitz* reached harbour, despite the damage inflicted by twenty-one shell hits as well as torpedo strikes. This kept her in the dockyard for three months, but contrasts favourably with the total loss of three British battle cruisers to shellfire in the same action.

The introduction of gunnery director firing in the Royal Navy came when *Thunderer*, the only ship so equipped, scored six times as many hits in practice than the next most successful ship. By 1914 only eight ships had been so fitted, but by Jutland all save *Erin* and *Agincourt* had been modified. There the gunnery of the four Queen Elizabeth class ships of the Fifth Battle Squadron was especially accurate. However,

Side view of HMS *Thunderer* circa 1914. The picture shows its two 13.5 inch gun turrets.

German range finding was better in poor visibility because of the advantage conferred by their more complex stereoscopic system.

Rather than the big guns mounted by the battleships, the mine and the torpedo appeared to be the greatest threat. There was early evidence of this when *Audacious* sank after striking a single mine off the coast of Ireland in 1914. She was the only dreadnought to be lost in this way. Three German ships: *Ostfriesland, Kronprinz* and *Bayern*, all struck mines in the Baltic, but survived. So too did the battle cruisers *Yavuz* (formerly *Goeben*) and *Inflexible* in the Black Sea and the Dardanelles. The torpedo did not account for a single dreadnought. *Marlborough, Moltke, Westfalen* and *Grosser Kurfürst* all survived torpedo attacks. However, it was the fear of German submarines which caused Jellicoe to turn away at Jutland and not risk a night action.

The German bases in the Heligoland Bight, at Wilhelmshaven on the Jade, at Cuxhaven, Emden and Brunsbüttel, were in a highly defensible position, and were linked by the Ems–Jade Canal, with the newly widened Kaiser Wilhelm Canal giving direct access to the Baltic port of Kiel. (The Baltic could be regarded as a reasonably secure training and working-up area.) To blockade these in the way in which Admiral Cornwallis had blockaded Brest during the French Revolutionary War in 1795, would have exposed modern ships to quite unacceptable hazards. A policy of distant blockade had to be applied by the Royal Navy, of necessity allowing the German ships some freedom of action in the North Sea, but denying them passage to the Atlantic where they could menace the ocean trade routes. In practice two factors reduced somewhat the opportunities afforded to the High Seas Fleet. The battle squadrons could only cross the bars of the Elbe and Weser at high tide and good naval intelligence work by the Admiralty gave warning of German intentions. The capture of a German codebook after the sinking of the cruiser *Magdeburg* in the Baltic gave the cipher experts an advantage, so that when Jellicoe took the Grand Fleet to sea in May 1916 it was in the confident knowledge that Admiral Scheer was about to sortie in force.

The older British bases of Plymouth, Portsmouth and Chatham, while well-placed for wars against the older enemies of Spain, Holland or France, were not suitable for hostilities against Germany in the North Sea. In 1903 the decision was taken to establish a base at Rosyth, but this was not entirely satisfactory. It appeared to be too easy to mine the approaches to the Forth, where there was not sufficient anchorage for a fleet. In addition, the Forth Bridge was vulnerable to an attack whose destruction could keep the fleet bottled up. A second base and anchorage was established at Invergordon on the Moray Firth, but a major fleet base with full repair and replenishment facilities was urgently needed. Scapa Flow in the Orkneys was to be the answer as it offered sufficient space and shelter and was well placed to control the northern exits from the North Sea into the Atlantic. In August 1914, however, it was still undefended, lacking booms, nets and searchlights, and early in the war the Grand Fleet was withdrawn to Lough Swilly in Ireland for its own safety. Nevertheless, it was at Scapa Flow that Admiral Jellicoe, appointed commander-in-chief on the eve of war, hoisted his flag in command of the Grand Fleet.

The Grand Fleet comprised twenty dreadnought battleships, a squadron of eight King Edward class and another of the five remaining Duncan class; at Invergordon was the 1st Battle Cruiser Squadron comprising, *Lion, Queen Mary, Princess Royal* and *New Zealand* under Admiral David Beatty. Sixteen cruisers and seventy-six destroyers (thirty-five of the latter based at Harwich) provided the scouting force and anti-torpedo screen. The Channel was guarded by HMS *Dreadnought* and the two Lord Nelson class ships, along with twenty-three pre-dreadnoughts of the Majestic, Canopus, London and Formidable classes, which initially ensured the safe passage to France of the British Expeditionary Force.

Swiftsure and *Triumph* were in the Pacific, *Australia* was in her home waters and *Invincible* was at Queenstown. The 2nd Battle Cruiser Squadron was in the Mediterranean, together with five armoured cruisers, chiefly to maintain a watch on the German battle cruiser *Goeben*. She was able to elude them and, with her attendant light cruiser *Breslau* to reach Constantinople where they were sold to Turkey, though remaining under the command of Admiral Wilhelm Souchon and manned still by their German crew. There they remained throughout the war, a threat to communications in the Levant and the Black Sea. Turkey had been assiduously courted by Germany in the previous decade, and the acquisition of *Goeben* (renamed *Yavuz Sultan Selim*) together with the loss of the two ships commandeered by the Admiralty, now brought her into the war.

By October 1914, Jellicoe's margin of superiority had vanished. With the loss of *Audacious*, with *Princess Royal* in dry dock and with problems rendering four more ships unserviceable, he had fifteen battleships and three battle cruisers against the fifteen and four of his opponents. The arrival of *Erin* and *Agincourt*, the completion of *Benbow*, *Emperor of India* and *Tiger*, together with the return of the four ships under repair, restored the advantage before the Germans were aware that it had been lost.

At this point the attention was switched to distant waters. The German Pacific Squadron of armoured and light cruisers under Admiral von Spee soon lost its base at Kiaochow to the Japanese, but contrived to remain a real threat to convoys. Off Coronel they met and overwhelmed Rear Admiral Sir Christopher Cradock's weaker ships. The loss of the two old armoured cruisers *Good Hope* and *Monmouth* did not in any way affect the overall balance of naval power, but the psychological blow was immense. At once the Admiralty acted, sending a hastily assembled squadron of two battle cruisers and five armoured cruisers under Admiral Sturdee. They encountered von Spee off the Falkland Islands and in a classic battle cruiser action *Inflexible* and *Invincible* outpaced, outranged and sank both *Scharnhorst* and *Gneisenau* while the armoured cruisers, *Bristol, Kent, Carnarvon* and *Cornwall*, similarly outclassed and sank the light cruisers *Leipzig, Nürnberg* and *Dresden*.

This seemed to justify the battle cruiser concept at a time when the fast battleships of the Queen Elizabeth class might have discredited it. The battle cruisers also sank three German light cruisers in the Heligoland Bight in 1914. The German admirals seem to have anticipated a close blockade by the Grand Fleet, to which their response would be attacks to whittle down the strength of their opponent, but in August 1914 a raid by Commodore Reginald Tyrwhitt's Harwich Force drew out a squadron of light cruisers into the range of the five ships of Admiral Beatty's 1st Battle Cruiser Squadron, *Mainz, Ariadne* and *Köln* being sunk.

German raids on Hartlepool, Scarborough and Whitby brought Beatty's battle cruisers south to Rosyth late in 1914. When a raid in January 1915 by Admiral Franz von Hipper's 1st Scouting Group of four battle cruisers was identified in advance by the codebreakers in Room 40, an interception was made, but the results were disappointing. Although with a five to four advantage in ships, higher speed and heavier guns, only the weakest of the German ships, the *Blücher* of 15,840 tons and armed with 8.2-inch guns, was sunk. Other aspects of the battle had a greater significance: a signal misunderstanding left *Moltke* unengaged and able to fire unimpeded. *Lion* was hit by three 12-inch shells from *Derfflinger* and then by a fourth which slowed her so that Beatty lost his control over the squadron. A hit on *Seydlitz* penetrated her magazines, but prompt action led to them being flooded and the ship saved. This led to corrective action being taken, action of which the British were unaware, leaving their ships vulnerable.

In the summer of 1916 came the long-awaited clash between the battle fleets. Again, intelligence gave Jellicoe the information that Scheer was planning a major sortie, and so the Grand Fleet put to sea with all available ships. Jellicoe had twenty-four battleships, his entire strength apart from *Royal Sovereign* which had only just joined the fleet and *Queen Elizabeth* which was undergoing a refit. In addition he had under his command the three Invincible class ships of the

3rd Battle Cruiser Squadron, at Scapa Flow for gunnery practice. To replace them, Beatty at Rosyth had the four new ships of the Fifth Battle Squadron, the 15-inch gunned *Warspite, Barham, Valiant* and *Malaya*, along with the six vessels of the 1st and 2nd Battle Cruiser Squadrons.

It was the light cruiser HMS *Galatea*, part of Beatty's scouting force, which first sighted the enemy, making contact with Hipper's Scouting Group. In the ensuing gun duel, first *Indefatigable* was hit by a salvo from *Von der Tann*, and then *Queen Mary* was struck by shells from *Derfflinger*. Both British ships blew up and sank. The flagship *Lion* was only saved from a similar fate by the flooding of a magazine after she had been hit in Q turret amidships.

By now the 15-inch guns of the Fifth Battle Squadron were dealing some heavy blows, and *Moltke, Von der Tann, Seydlitz* and *Lützow* were all badly hit during the run south. The leading ships of Scheer's battle fleet were then sighted, and Beatty turned northwards to draw the High Seas Fleet under the guns of Jellicoe's battle squadrons. Unfortunately, another signals failure led to this order not being relayed to Vice Admiral Sir Hugh Evan-Thomas, so that the *Warspite* was badly hit as she continued southwards. Jellicoe, now at last in full awareness of the presence of Scheer as well as Hipper, deployed his ships from a cruising formation in four columns of line abreast into a line ahead, crossing the T of the German fleet. At this point another disaster struck. HMS *Invincible*, at the head of the line, was hit amidships and became the third of the battle cruisers to be destroyed by an explosion.

A major fleet action, at so great a disadvantage of numbers was not Scheer's intention, and he ordered his ships to execute the 'battle turn away together' and break off the fight. A second, and even briefer flurry of action saw Jellicoe turn away, fearing torpedo attack, and some confused fighting during the night ended this opportunity for a decisive fleet action to rival Trafalgar.

Battlecruiser HMS *Invincible* in 1911–12 at anchor. (© *National Maritime Museum, Greenwich, London*)

Apart from the three battle cruisers, the Royal Navy lost three armoured cruisers and eight destroyers. The High Seas Fleet lost the battle cruiser *Lützow* when, after a long fight to save the battered ship, her crew was taken off and she was sunk by torpedo. The pre-dreadnought *Pommern*, along with four light cruisers and five torpedo boats were lost and, on the basis of these figures, the Germans on reaching the safety of their port, claimed a victory. Equally, on the basis that the Germans had withdrawn and left the Grand fleet in control, the Admiralty could also claim a victory. Their fleet was ready for sea again after replenishing fuel and shells. Only HMS *Marlborough* of Jellicoe's fleet, hit by a torpedo, was in need of extensive repair. All other major damage had been suffered by Beatty's squadrons, but even he retained a numerical advantage over Hipper. All of the German battle cruisers had suffered heavy damage. Apart from the loss of

Lützow, all of *Von der Tann*'s turrets had been put out of action and *Seydlitz* reached port in a sinking condition. Some units of the High Seas Fleet were in dockyard hands for months.

Of the ships planned or under construction at the time of Jutland, few were completed, and fewer still saw service. In Britain the Cabinet decided that no more capital ships were to be laid down after 1915, hence Fisher's designation of the three ships of the Courageous class as 'large light cruisers'. Intended for a not-entirely-planned assault on Germany's Baltic coast, each was of some 23,000 tons, of relatively shallow draught, and were intended to mount two of the new 18-inch guns. In fact, to get *Courageous* and *Glorious* into service in 1917, each was armed with two twin 15-inch turrets; they did see action against German light forces in the Heligoland Bight in November 1917, but without success. HMS *Furious* was armed with the 18-inch guns, but by the end of 1917 had begun conversion to an aircraft carrier. HMS *Hood*, one of four planned 15-inch battle cruisers of 45,000 tons, was laid down in 1916, but was not completed until 1920. The other three vessels were cancelled.

HMS *Hood*.

Germany did complete the 15-inch battleships, *Bayern* and *Baden* and the 12-inch battle cruiser *Hindenburg* in 1916–17, but the later battleships, *Sachsen* and *Württemberg* and the battle cruisers *Mackensen* and *Graf Spee*, were never completed.

The United States completed six more battleships during the war, of which *New York* and *Texas* formed part of the Sixth Battle Squadron at Scapa Flow, but none of the six saw action. Japan also extended her battle fleet by the *Ise* and *Hyuga* by 1918.

Elsewhere the tale is one of cancellation throughout. None of the French battleships of the Normandie class were completed and the four Lyon class battle cruisers were cancelled. Italy cancelled the four Caracciolo class and Russia the four Borodino class. Four Austrian Tegetthoff class were never laid down.

Though the assertion that the German fleet never put to sea again is untrue, it never again risked action. As an American observer put it 'the German fleet has assaulted its jailer, but is back in its cell'. When it was ordered to sortie again in November 1918, the crews mutinied. The distant blockade, maintained by the battle squadrons at Scapa Flow had proved to have a decisive effect on the war. It was necessarily a lengthy process, as Germany was much less dependent on sea-borne trade than Britain, but by 1918 the effects were beginning to tell. By restricting the High Seas Fleet to the North Sea, the Royal Navy was able to prevent any large-scale surface threat to the main arteries of trade, while the German inability to break this stranglehold led directly to the decision to initiate unrestricted submarine warfare, which in turn had led eventually to the American entry into the war in 1917. A Sixth Battle Squadron of American dreadnoughts arrived at Scapa Flow, more to emphasise the reality of the alliance than because they were needed. Of much greater significance were the escorts protecting the vital Atlantic convoys of supplies and the passage of the American Expeditionary Force for the final decisive battles of the autumn of 1918.

The absence of any other major action meant that the battle fleets had an uneventful existence for the rest of the war. For many of the great ships, which had been the index of the naval strength of Britain and Germany in the pre-war years, the only glimpse of the enemy had been through the murk of cloud and smoke at Jutland. The German *König* was involved in an unequal action in the Baltic with the old Russian battleship *Slava*, which was disabled and later scuttled. HMS *Dreadnought* rammed and sank a U-boat when on patrol in the North Sea. In neither in the Mediterranean, the Adriatic nor the Black Sea was there any battleship action, though *Yavuz Sultan Selim* (formerly *Goeben*) did bombard Sebastopol, and was on three occasions in action with Russian ships. Japan lost *Kawachi* by internal explosion in Tokoyuma Bay in July 1918.

Chapter Seven

Pre-dreadnoughts in the First World War

Except in two instances, the pre-dreadnoughts of all combatant navies were relegated to secondary duties during the war but nevertheless suffered heavy losses. The German Admiral Franz Mauve, commanding the 2nd Battle Squadron of the High Seas Fleet, pleaded for his five Deutschland class to be included in the 1916 sortie which led to the battle of Jutland. There *Pommern* was torpedoed and lost when her secondary magazine exploded, as it was badly placed and inadequately protected.

The Anglo-French Naval Agreement had envisaged the French fleet remaining in the Mediterranean, but there it was joined by several squadrons of British pre-dreadnoughts; together they formed the fleet for the bold, but eventually disastrous Gallipoli campaign. This, as originally planned, anticipated a naval assault through the Dardanelles to the Bosphorus where, with Constantinople under its guns, the Turks would be forced to surrender and a supply route opened through the Black Sea to Russia. This would inevitably lead to naval losses, but among a category of ships of limited usefulness. When, after a preliminary bombardment of the Turkish positions, the attempt was made to force the passage of the Dardanelles it met with disaster. HMS *Ocean* and HMS *Irresistible* were mined; HMS *Goliath* and HMS *Majestic* were torpedoed, and the French battleship *Bouvet* was also mined, sinking in a matter of minutes, while HMS *Albion* was damaged by shellfire from the forts.

These disasters led to a change of plan, with abortive military landings. Fully alerted, the Turks had ample time to prepare defensive

French battleship *Bouvet*.

positions and bring in reinforcements. In addition, the new battleship
HMS *Queen Elizabeth*, sent to calibrate her guns, and the battle cruiser
HMS *Inflexible* were quickly removed from the danger zone. There
were no further major naval actions in the Mediterranean, but a steady
stream of losses.

Numbers of the pre-dreadnoughts of the Royal Navy were assigned
to the Channel Fleet in 1914, helping to cover the passage of the BEF

HMS *Queen Elizabeth*.

to France. These included *Majestic, Canopus, Venerable, Queen*, and *Lord Nelson*. The remaining Majestic class were all deployed in 1914 as guard ships in the east coast ports, but in 1915 the main armament was removed from *Mars, Magnificent, Hannibal* and *Victorious*, and used to equip the new monitors of the General Wolfe class. The disarmed ships were use as troop transports, store ships and depot ships. *Illustrious*, guard ship for the Tyne and Humber, also became a store ship, while *Prince George* returned from the Dardanelles to become the depot ship at Chatham. Only two remained in active service in 1918: *Caesar* in the

HMS *Caesar*. (© *National Maritime Museum, Greenwich, London*)

West Indies, and *Jupiter*, after use as an icebreaker on the Murmansk route, was sent to the East Indies.

In 1914 the six ships of the Canopus class formed the 8th Battle Squadron, part of the Channel Fleet. *Canopus* herself was detached to the South American station, where she fired the first shots of the Battle of the Falkland Islands. *Glory* was stationed first in American and West Indian waters, then in the Mediterranean and finally at Murmansk. The others were all sent to the Dardanelles in 1915, where *Ocean* was mined and *Goliath* sunk by torpedo. *Vengeance* remained as guard ship

Battleship HMS *Goliath*. (© *National Maritime Museum, Greenwich, London*)

HMS *Ocean* in 1900. (*Richard Perkins collection*, © *National Maritime Museum, Greenwich, London*)

HMS *Formidable*.

HMS *Irresistible*, abandoned and sinking after hitting an exploding mine during the Battle of Gallipoli, 18 March 1915.

at Alexandria and *Albion* returned to home waters and to guard ship duties on the east coast.

Of the next class to be built, *Irresistible* was mined in the Dardanelles and *Formidable* sunk by U-24. *Implacable* survived Gallipoli and served first in the Adriatic and later in the East Indies. *Bulwark*, of the later London class blew up in 1914 off Sheerness, a victim of unstable cordite; the other four survived not only the Dardanelles but the war itself. In 1917 *London* was converted to a mine-laying role, while *Venerable*, *Queen* and *Prince of Wales* remained in the Adriatic.

The five remaining ships of the Duncan class (the unfortunate *Montagu* had been wrecked on Lundy in 1906) formed the 6th Battle Squadron in 1914, and saw extensive service in home waters and in the Mediterranean. *Russell* was mined and sunk off Malta in 1916, and *Cornwallis* fell victim to the torpedoes of U–32 the following January, also off Malta. The others, *Exmouth*, *Duncan* and *Albermarle* all survived the war.

HMS *Implacable* at anchor at Spithead. (© *National Maritime Museum, Greenwich, London*)

The eight ships of the King Edward VII class (derisively known as the 'wobbly eight') formed the 3rd Battle Squadron of the Grand Fleet in 1914, but never saw action as a squadron. In 1916 the name ship was mined off Cape Wrath and two days before the Armistice *Britannia* was torpedoed by U–50 off Cape Trafalgar. Both ships were lost after lengthy struggles to save them. *Hibernia* and *Zealandia* (renamed in 1911 when her original name was transferred to the battle cruiser *New Zealand*) both survived the Gallipoli operation, while *Hindustan* was in 1918 the depot ship for the raid on Zeebrugge.

HMS *Commonwealth* ended her career as a gunnery training ship until, with her five remaining sisters, she was sent to the breakers' yards

Battleship HMS *Bulwark*. (© *National Maritime Museum, Greenwich, London*)

Battleship HMS *Queen*. (© *National Maritime Museum, Greenwich, London*)

in 1921. *Lord Nelson* and *Agamemnon* were stationed in the Channel and then in the Mediterranean. The oldest capital ship to fire her guns in the war was the old *Revenge* of 1892 which, now renamed *Redoutable* to free her original name for a new ship, bombarded German positions on the Belgian coast in October 1914.

Chapter Eight

The Treaty of Versailles and the Washington Naval Treaty

The long-awaited day of decision in the North Sea came in an unexpected way. The long-term effects of the blockade, the failure of Ludendorff's spring offensive in 1918 and the success of the allied counter-offensive, together with the collapse of her allies and civil disturbances at home led to the abdication of the Kaiser and the request for an armistice in 1918. The allied terms involved the surrender of most of Germany's modern warships, along with aircraft, artillery, lorries and railway rolling stock, to ensure that if peace negotiations proved difficult, she would be in no position to reopen hostilities. The allies demanded the surrender of eleven battleships of the Kaiser, König and Baden classes, the six remaining battle cruisers, eight light cruisers, fifty destroyers and all U-boats. After some debate, it was decided that the surface ships would be interned at Scapa Flow and the submarines at Harwich, neutral Norway and Spain having refused to take responsibility for them. Most were surrendered on 21 November 1918 and were escorted to Scapa Flow. There the order of Admiral Beatty, now Commander-in-Chief of the Grand Fleet, was that 'the German ensign will be lowered at sunset, and will not be hoisted again without permission'. *König* and the light cruiser *Dresden* were in dry dock, and arrived in December, and *Baden* later. The greater part of the crews were repatriated, leaving only skeleton crews on board.

The Big Three at Versailles readily agreed on the need to restrict Germany's naval as well as her military strength. She was to be allowed no submarines or dreadnoughts and her navy was to be reduced to the level of a coast defence force, with six old battleships, all over ten years old. Replacements were to be permitted when the ships would be over twenty years old, and were limited to 10,000 tons displacement – heavy cruiser size. The six comprised *Zähringen*, completed in 1902, and converted into a target ship in 1926, *Preussen, Elsass* and *Hessen* of the Braunschweig class, and *Schleswig-Holstein* and *Schliessen* of the Deutschland class. The first three were eventually replaced by the three 'pocket battleships' in the first stage of Germany's rearmament, while *Hessen* was converted into a radio-controlled target ship in 1931. *Schleswig-Holstein* and *Schliessen* were still in service in 1939, and were eventually destroyed by bombing in 1944–5. *Lothringen, Braunschweig* and *Hannover* were retained as unarmed depot ships.

The disposal of the German dreadnoughts presented a greater problem. Initially it was proposed that the eight ships of the Nassau and Helgoland classes, which had not been surrendered at the Armistice, should be sunk in deep water. There were proposals for a division of the spoils and France, in particular, showed an interest in putting some of the captured ships into service. The Americans favoured the destruction of all the High Seas Fleet. The Germans themselves solved the problem. On 21 June 1919, when the ships of the Royal Navy's 1st Battle Squadron had put to sea for gunnery practice, the order was given to the crews to scuttle the ships. Fifteen of the sixteen capital ships were sunk, and *Baden* was only saved by being beached in a sinking condition.

This put an end to the debate, and it was decided to divide out the remaining ships, with the proviso that they were to be scrapped, or rendered unfit for service, within eighteen months. Five light cruisers and ten destroyers were allowed for inclusion into each of the French and Italian navies. The ships scuttled at Scapa Flow were reckoned as part of Britain's share and the work of raising them and breaking them up continued over two decades. Twelve had been disposed of by

1939, and from 1962 the salvage of phosphor-bronze from the screws of *König, Markgraf* and *Kronprinz Wilhelm* began. *Baden* was sunk by gunfire as a target vessel in 1921 and the four Nassau class, *Helgoland* and *Oldenburg* were broken up. *Thüringen* was used as a target vessel by the French before she too was broken up, a fate planned also for *Ostfriesland* at American hands. In 1921 she was used as a target in Chesapeake Bay to determine the vulnerability of battleships to air attack. Careful arrangements were made to control the experiment, allowing for a series of attacks, with predetermined bomb loads, after each of which observers would board the ships to assess the damage. General Billy Mitchell was intent on proving the superiority of aircraft, and after the first wave had resulted in only three hits from the eleven 500 pound bombs dropped, he ordered the second wave to deliver their 1,000 pound bombs in succession. There were no hits, but a near miss under her quarter caused such damage that she sank within minutes.

SMS *Ostfriesland*.

A great dispute then arose as to the lessons to be learnt from this episode. The advocates of air power – and there were many – hailed the end of the battleship era. Brigadier General Billy Mitchell, who sought the creation of an independent air force in the USA, led what was described as 'a hysterical crusade' before overreaching himself and making allegations which led to his court-martial. Admiral William Sims also contended that air power would change the pattern of war at sea. He foresaw that 'carrier-borne aircraft will sweep the enemy fleet clean of its airplanes, and proceed to bomb the battleships and torpedo them'.

Admiral John 'Jacky' Fisher in England also saw the aircraft carrier as 'the capital ship of the future'. Traditionalists were not convinced. They pointed out that *Ostfriesland* was not under way, that her guns were not manned and that she had no damage control parties on board – in short, that she was an open and unrepresentative target. Against this it was argued that as her magazines were empty and her boilers not fired up, she was less likely to explode if hit. Bombing tests carried out in 1924 on the hull of the incomplete battleship *Washington* failed to sink her, so the lesson there appeared to be that modern ships, with better underwater protection, could survive against air attack, even discounting the absence of any anti-aircraft weapons.

For the moment, however, the main issue was that of disarmament. One of Woodrow Wilson's Fourteen Points had been 'the reduction of armaments to the lowest point consistent with domestic security'. Germany had already been disarmed by the treaty; now the League of Nations was beginning to discuss a wider disarmament. The powers had reduced their forces from the inflated size of the war years. In the immediate aftermath of the war, Britain had begun to scrap her older warships. The oldest battleships still in service were the Majestic class, four of which had been disarmed in 1915. These were now sold for scrap, as were all the remaining twenty-one pre-dreadnoughts with the exception of *Agamemnon*, retained as a target ship until

1926. *Dreadnought* herself was deleted from the list in 1920 and sold for £44,000 to the breakers in 1924. *Erin* and *Agincourt* were placed in reserve in 1919, and, after an attempt to sell the latter to Brazil, both were scrapped in 1922, while HMS *Canada* resumed her original identity as *Almirante Latorre* under Chilean colours.

This left Britain with twenty-nine dreadnoughts in service, the most modern being the battle cruiser *Hood*. She had been laid down in September 1916, supposedly embodying all the lessons learnt at Jutland, and had joined the fleet in 1920. At 45,200 tons, with eight 15-inch guns and capable of 31 knots, she was cherished by the press as 'the mighty *Hood*' in the inter-war years, so that her destruction in 1941 was a profound shock. Three sister ships, *Anson*, *Howe* and *Rodney* had been cancelled in 1917 before building work had begun. The post war building plans were for four battle cruisers designated G3 with the intended names of *Invincible*, *Inflexible*, *Indomitable* and *Indefatigable*. These were to displace 48,000 tons and were to mount nine 16-inch guns in three triple turrets, two forward and one immediately aft of the bridge. Further plans existed for four battleships of 43,500 tons with nine 18-inch guns, similarly disposed but these were never laid down.

The United States had continued with her building programme of two battleships each year during the war and the 1914 programme had included a third ship, *Idaho*, paid for by the sale of *Mississippi* and the old *Idaho* to Greece. By 1919 she had seventeen dreadnoughts in commission, as well as twenty-three older battleships. Two more, *Tennessee* and *California* were ready in 1921, by which time the 16-inch gun *Maryland* was completed. In a massive building programme, three more of the Maryland class were being built, and six South Dakota class of 42,300 tons, each armed with twelve 16-inch guns, had been laid down. In addition there were plans for America's first battle cruisers, initially to be of 35,000 tons and with a design speed of 35 knots deriving from twenty-four boilers, requiring seven funnels. Modified plans gave a displacement of 43,500 tons, with eight 16-inch guns in place of the original ten 14-inch, and a more conventional two-funnelled profile. These Lexington class battle cruisers were laid down in 1920–21.

Japan also had a major building programme. After the loss of *Kawachi* she had nine dreadnoughts in commission in 1918, and was building her first two 16-inch gunned ships, *Nagato* and *Mutsu*. Her 8/8 plan, devised as early as 1910, envisaged a fleet of eight modern battleships and eight battle cruisers, with a replacement age of only eight years. The next four ships in this scheme were laid down in 1920. These were *Tosa* and *Kaga*, 38,500 ton battleships with ten 16-inch guns; the battle cruisers *Amagi* and *Akagi* of 47,000 tons, a similar armament and with a speed of 30 knots. Two more Amagis and four fast Owari class battleships would complete the plan. It was clear that a new, Pacific-based naval race had begun.

With sixteen ships projected against Britain's eight, the Americans were aiming at parity by 1924. However, Japanese ambitions in the Far East were causing great concern to both leading powers. With her acquisition of Germany's Pacific islands north of the Equator under mandate, and after her 'Twenty-one demands' to China, it was clear that Japan was seeking a domination of the Pacific unacceptable to either the USA or Britain, despite the existence of the 1902 Anglo-Japanese alliance. Exacerbating this, financial problems and industrial depression began to affect both western powers in the post-war years. When, therefore, the British Government indicated unofficially to the USA its willingness to accept parity of naval strength, an arms limitation conference was convened at Washington to discuss details.

The Americans brought to the conference table more far-reaching proposals than had been anticipated. They proposed to cancel all fifteen of their capital ships under construction, together with fifteen pre-dreadnoughts, a total of almost 850,000 tons. In return they would require Britain to cancel the four G3 plan Invincible class and to scrap nineteen older dreadnoughts of almost 600,000 tons. Japan would respond by disposing of ten pre-dreadnoughts, and cancelling the seven ships under construction and those planned – 450,000 tons in all. In addition a 'battleship holiday' was proposed which, by putting a stop to new naval construction, would maintain the balance of naval strength between the three powers. The implications went deeper than these initial proposals, as Britain had already begun the run-down of her battle fleet, with twenty-nine pre-dreadnoughts (430,000 tons) and four dreadnoughts (97,000 tons) already destined for the breakers' yards. Furthermore, while America had the largest number of ships under construction, those of the South Dakota class were not even half-built and the Lexington class ships barely laid-down. The Japanese were reluctant to accept numerical inferiority and Britain was aware that acceptance of the American proposals would leave her with an apparent equality, but comprising rather older ships.

The eventual agreement saw an acceptance of the broad principles, but with some modification to detail. The 'battleship holiday' was accepted – no new ships were to be built for ten years, and then they would be limited to 35,000 tons and mount guns of no more than 16-inch calibre (an increase to 18-inch had been planned for Japan's *Owari*). The replacement age was set at twenty years, with the oldest remaining ships being the American *Utah* (1911) the Japanese *Kongo* (1913) and the British *Iron Duke* (1914). It would be the early 30s before new construction could begin. Japanese doubts were allayed by the consideration that her involvement was limited to the Pacific, while the USA had to maintain an Atlantic fleet, and that British commitments were worldwide. In addition, an undertaking was given that no new naval bases were to be constructed in the Pacific. This prevented the Americans from fortifying a base in the Philippines (then an American protectorate) and Britain from doing the same at Hong Kong. This left the USA with Pearl Harbor in the Hawaiian Islands and Britain with Singapore, as their advance bases.

Britain was to be allowed to build two 16-inch gun battleships to match those in the American and Japanese fleets. Meanwhile the retained strength was set at 600,000 tons for Britain (twenty-two ships, to be increased on the completion of the two new ships); 500,000 tons for the USA (eighteen ships) and 300,000 tons for Japan (ten ships). France and Italy were each allowed 175,000 tons total and were to retain some of their pre-dreadnoughts, as neither had more than six dreadnoughts in commission. The earliest date for replacement of their older ships was to be 1927.

There was a proposal that the 5:5:3 ratio should apply also to aircraft carriers, with tonnages of 80,000 tons for Britain and America, and 48,000 tons for Japan. The Royal Navy had already built or converted four ships for a total of 81,000 tons. These were *Argus* (laid down as the liner *Conto Rosso*), *Furious*, under conversion from her original light battle cruiser design, and *Hermes*, the first carrier to be designed and built as such. *Eagle* had been restored to Chile as the battleship *Almirante Latorre*, while other wartime conversions had either been disposed of, re-converted or were in use as depot ships.

As the Americans wished to convert two of their Lexington class to carriers, it was eventually agreed that each of the three major naval powers could convert two hulls without limitations, but that otherwise a maximum displacement of 27,000 tons would be permitted and a total tonnage of 135,000 tons for Britain and the USA, with 80,000 tons for Japan and 60,000 each for Italy and France. Existing ships were to be regarded as experimental and could be replaced at any time, otherwise a replacement age of twenty years was agreed. The conversion of *Lexington* and *Saratoga* into 33,000 ton carriers was therefore begun, and Japan decided upon a similar conversion of the two Amagi class. Damage to the hull of *Amagi* before the launch led to her being scrapped, and the work transferred to the battleship hull *Kaga*. The Royal Navy similarly converted the former 'large light cruisers' *Courageous* and *Glorious* and the French converted the *Bearn*.

Disposal of the other hulls then building continued, with the Japanese *Tosa* and the American *Washington* being sunk as target vessels. Britain converted two of the G3 battle cruisers into the two 16-inch gunned battleships she was allowed. These were the *Nelson* and *Rodney* which were restricted to 35,000 tons. The original design had been for 48,000 tons. The displacement did not include fuel nor reserve feed water, which gave the designers rather more scope, enabling them to incorporate the liquids into the anti-torpedo defence as a damping layer between the armour and the ships' vitals. Nevertheless, the reduction in displacement had to be made and the choice, as ever, lay between armour, guns and speed. In practice this was easily resolved, as the vessels were to be battleships with hitting power and defensive armour the priorities. The saving was made in the engine rooms, and they were relatively slow at 23 knots. This however was faster than their American contemporaries (20.5 k) and only a little slower than the Nagatos (25 k). Their main armament was concentrated forward of the

HMS *Nelson*.

bridge in three triple turrets, B turret being superimposed over A, and giving six guns able to fire forward and all nine on the broadside. This concentration of the main armament, and therefore the magazines, reduced the extent of the central citadel and its armour. The secondary armament was similarly concentrated aft, partly compensating for the reduced arc of fire of the main armament, which could not extend much aft of the beam without causing blast damage to the ships themselves.

Until *Nelson* and *Rodney* were commissioned in 1927 the Royal Navy retained twenty-two capital ships, but then four had to go. The oldest, *Thunderer*, had been converted into a cadet training ship in 1920 and was now scrapped, along with two of the remaining ships of the King George V class. The third, *Centurion*, was to have an extended career which began with her conversion, her main armament removed, into a remotely-controlled target ship. Japan's oldest dreadnought, *Settsu*, also became a target ship, but she had only to scrap her four oldest ships to stay within the treaty limits, as had the Americans, while Britain had to lose nineteen.

Further reduction of the fleets was to take place in the early 1930s. The four ships of the Iron Duke class were taken out of service in 1931, and three of them were scrapped, along with the battle cruiser *Tiger*. *Iron Duke* was reduced to a gunnery training ship, with the removal of two of her five turrets, her armoured belt and a reduction in her engine power. Japan similarly demilitarised *Hiei* and the Americans, *Wyoming* and *Utah*, and *Florida* was scrapped. This left the USA and Britain with fifteen capital ships each by 1935, while the Japanese had nine. The limitation treaties had at least ensured that there could never again be a battle fleet action on the scale of Jutland.

Chapter Nine

Rearmament

The reduced battle fleets could not be augmented in numbers, but two significant developments followed from the Washington treaty. The first of these has already been covered – the conversion of some of the cancelled ships into aircraft carriers. Although the dispute over the relative merits of the big gun and naval aircraft had yet to be resolved, the commissioning of carriers into the major navies had begun. This led inevitably to the perception of the need to provide battleships with the means to survive an air attack. Anti-aircraft armament was added to other improvements, including the conversion of coal-burning vessels to oil fuel, improved protection and the provision of catapult-launched spotter aircraft, all of which combined to make the older ships vastly more effective. In some cases the result was a complete transformation of a ship which had served throughout the First World War, into an essential unit of the battle fleet in the second.

Nowhere was this done more thoroughly than in Japan. The ships which she had been allowed to retain had to be of maximum effectiveness and the work done on the four Kongo class amounted to little short of a complete rebuild. During two periods of conversion they were transformed from 1914 battle cruisers into fast battleships well-suited to the role of escorts to the carrier strike force. Among other modifications, the total weight of armour was increased from 6,500 tons to over 10,000 tons, and the ships were completely re-engined. They were also given the 'pagoda' bridge which became so characteristic of Japanese battleships and had two funnels in place of the original three.

Japanese battle-cruiser *Kongo*.

The four old battleships were given similar, if less extensive, treatment, and even the two Nagato class were refitted. In particular the elevation of their 16-inch guns was increased from 30 to 43 degrees for added range. All the ships were converted from coal to oil, increasing their efficiency, but also increasing their country's dependence on external oil supplies.

In America one outward sign of refit was the replacement of the familiar lattice masts by those of a more conventional pattern. Here too the conversion to oil fuel from coal, and the reduction in the number of funnels from two to one gave the ships a more modern profile. This was repeated in the Royal Navy's Queen Elizabeth class whose two funnels were trunked into one during the 20s. *Repulse* and *Renown* were given improved armour and, in the case of *Renown*, an anti-torpedo bulge and a tower bridge of the type introduced into *Nelson*. In all the ships the anti-aircraft armament was increased, but in all it was found to be

Battlecruiser HMS *Renown* in 1945 alongside at Devonport. (© *National Maritime Museum, Greenwich, London*)

inadequate to the needs of combat. After 1939 further installation of 20mm and 40mm weapons had to be made. The Revenge class vessels were less substantially modified and HMS *Hood*, due for refit in 1939, could not be spared when war came for the essential work to be carried out.

The first significant new building came in Germany, in a class of ships nominally within the treaty limits, but alarming in their size and hitting-power. These were the three armoured cruisers, known as Panzerschiffen in Germany, but revered elsewhere as 'pocket battleships' of the Deutschland class. Designated as the legitimate replacements for the three Braunschweig class, then serving as coast defence and depot ships, they were supposedly within the treaty limits of 10,000 tons displacement, made possible by the use of electric arc welding as opposed to traditional riveted plates. Although this method did save some fifteen per cent of the weight of the hull alone, they nevertheless exceeded the limit by 1,700 tons (3,000 tons at full load). Their armour was designed to give protection against the 8-inch guns permitted to cruisers under the Washington Treaty, while their diesel engines gave them an extensive radius of action and a speed of 28 knots. This was faster than any capital ship save the three British battle cruisers and the four Japanese Kongo class. Armed with six 11-inch guns in two triple turrets, they were more powerful than any cruiser, and seemed ideal as commerce raiders – they could outgun almost any vessel which could catch them.

The first Deutschland was ordered in 1928 and laid down in February 1929, under the Chancellorship of Gustav Stresemann, and the other two, *Admiral Scheer* and *Admiral Graf Spee*, were laid down

Panzerschiff *Admiral Graf Spee*.

in 1931–32 in the dying years of the Weimar Republic. By the time the first was commissioned in April 1933, Adolf Hitler had become Chancellor of Germany.

France and Italy, their eyes on one another as well as on Germany, both began to rearm. The 1930 London Naval Agreement extended the 'battleship holiday' to 1936, and retained the Washington limitations on displacement and armament, but neither France nor Italy was a signatory.

France needed new ships to replace the aging Danton class which were still in service in a limited role. She had lost one of her seven dreadnoughts when *France* ran aground in 1923. The building of *Deutschland* intensified her need and in 1932 work began on a battle cruiser of 26,500 tons and 30 knots. *Dunkerque* embodied one of the innovations which had been planned for the cancelled Normandie class and Lyon class, as her eight 13-inch guns were mounted in two quadruple turrets, both mounted forward of the bridge. They were more widely separated than those of the Royal Navy Nelson class, to reduce the chance of both turrets being put out of action by a single hit. The arc of fire was severely limited, as it was found impracticable to use the main armament more than a few degrees aft of the beam, and the light construction of the ship made her vulnerable to damage from the recoil of the guns. With twelve of the sixteen guns of the dual-purpose secondary armament also in quadruple mountings, and with a large aircraft hangar and crane aft, *Dunkerque* and her sister *Strasbourg* clearly belonged to a new generation of capital ships; the layout was retained in the next class of French ships.

Strasbourg was laid down in 1934, by which time Germany was building the two later Deutschland class, *Admiral Scheer* and *Admiral Graf Spee*. In the same year Italy laid down two new fast battleships. She too had only four battleships in service; attempts to salvage and refit the wreck of *Leonardo da Vinci* which had been sunk in 1916 by a magazine explosion, having been abandoned and *Dante Alighieri*

French battle-cruiser *Dunkerque*.

having been scrapped. *Littorio* and *Vittorio Veneto* were nominally of 35,000 tons, but displaced some 6,000 tons more, and were armed with nine 15-inch guns in triple mountings. Capable of 31 knots, they incorporated improvements to armour and anti-torpedo protection.

France countered these by laying down two 35,000 ton ships of the Richelieu class, whereupon Italy began two more of the Littorio class. A new naval race was under way. Britain had proposed a further conference to restrict naval building: it met in London in 1935, but

French battle-cruiser *Strasbourg*.

Italian battleship *Littorio*.

to little effect. The limit of 35,000 tons for battleships was ratified yet again, though the Italians were far exceeding it already, and an attempt to restrict the calibre of guns to 14-inch proved a failure. Both France and Italy were already building ships armed with 15-inch guns, while

Vittorio Veneto at Matapan.

the Americans retained the 16-inch and the Japanese went to 18.1-inch for the Yamato class battleships.

Italy began a very extensive modernisation of her four old battleships. This included the removal of the midships triple turret, enabling the installation of more powerful engines giving a speed of 27 knots, but protective armour, though improved, remained inadequate. The Italian fleet was developing in a way which caused no little concern to France and Britain after 1935. While Mussolini had been looked upon as an associate during the brief existence of the Stresa Front, (an agreement between the Italian Fascist dictator, and the French and British prime ministers), this concern had not been acute. However, the Italian invasion of Abyssinia revealed Mussolini's imperial ambitions; his new fleet was clearly intended to make the Mediterranean his longed for 'Mare Nostrum'. The involvement of both Mussolini and Hitler in active support for the Nationalist side during the Spanish Civil War, and the formation of the Rome-Berlin Axis, placed the two dictators firmly on the same side.

German battle-cruiser *Scharnhorst*.

German battle-cruiser *Gneisenau*.

Soon after coming to power in 1933, Hitler was determined to rebuild the German navy as an effective fighting force and he was disposed to listen to the request made to him by Admiral Raedar for the next two of the Panzerschiff programme to be better-protected and more heavily armed. An initial increase in displacement to 19,000 tons was agreed, but this was soon increased to 26,000, and *Scharnhorst* and *Gneisenau* exceeded even this by a further 6,000 tons. A third triple turret was added, but the calibre of gun remained 11-inch. This was an expedient to enable more rapid completion of the ships, using the six turrets built for the three further Deutschland class, but it left the two ships under-armed by comparison with their contemporaries in any navy. It was planned to replace the 11-inch turrets with 15-inch, when the German armament industry was again in full production, but this was never carried out. Nevertheless, the two ships were to be a serious threat to Britain's trade routes.

Britain's response to the renewed German naval building was the agreement that Germany could build up to thirty-five per cent of the

German battleship *Bismarck*.

Royal Navy's strength in surface ships with parity in submarines. The assumption that a freely-negotiated agreement would have a more binding effect than the imposition of a clearly unenforceable disarmed state gave Hitler and his admirals as much scope as they needed for the moment.

As Britain had fifteen capital ships in commission in 1935, Germany could build five, of which the Scharnhorst class included the first two. The next two were to follow quickly: the 15-inch *Bismarck* and *Tirpitz* were ordered in 1935 and 1936, and both were laid down in the latter year. Nominally of 35,000 tons, they displaced 41,700 and 42,900 respectively on completion. By then the maximum tonnage for battleships had risen to 45,000 tons by an agreement signed in 1938. They were powered by conventional turbines, giving a maximum speed of 29 knots, rather than by the diesels of the Deutschland class or the turbo-electric motors originally planned for them, and they were as well protected as any of the last generation of battleships.

They were the last two battleships to be built by Germany, though two more were laid down in 1939 out of six proposed by the Z Plan, by which, as in the early years of the century, Germany sought to attain parity with Britain. These were to be 55,000 ton ships armed with eight 16-inch guns – some of the guns were built and used in coastal batteries in Norway and on the Channel coast, but the ships were abandoned. The accompanying project for three 15-inch 35,000 ton battle cruisers never reached fruition, nor did a series of further battleship plans coded H41 to H44.

In face of this renewed challenge to Britain's overseas trade routes, the Admiralty prepared to begin building modern battleships in 1935. The 35,000 ton limit was still in force, and a proposal to limit the calibre of big guns to 14-inch was being canvassed, so that these were the specification for the five ships of the King George V class, the first two of which were authorised in 1936. In that year the London Naval Agreement did limit the calibre to 14-inch, but with the proviso that this would not be binding on the signatories if Japan failed to ratify

HMS *King George V*.

the treaty by April 1937. Not only did Japan refuse to sign, she had embarked on the 18-inch Yamato class, but Britain was committed to the 14-inch gun. The original intention had been to mount twelve of these in three quadruple turrets, but in the event, the number of barrels was reduced to ten by substituting a twin turret for the second forward quadruple mounting in order to save weight. This delayed the completion of the ships while the new turret was designed and problems over the complex quadruple turrets also postponed production. *King George V* joined the fleet in December 1940, *Prince of Wales* and *Duke of York* in 1941, and *Anson* and *Howe* in 1942. They displaced 38,000 tons in the final design, with 12,000 tons of armour and could raise 29 knots. A secondary armament of sixteen 5.25-inch dual-purpose guns, and between thirty-two and seventy-two 40mm Oerlikons showed the awareness of the need to provide for adequate defence against air attack.

USS *South Dakota.*

USS *Missouri*.

A design for four Lion class battleships of 40,000 tons was prepared and two keels were laid down, but construction work was abandoned when it became apparent that the need for cruisers, escorts and carriers was more urgent. One further battleship was built during the war, the 44,500 ton *Vanguard* armed with the four 15-inch twin turrets removed from *Courageous* and *Glorious* on their conversion to aircraft carriers, but she was not commissioned until 1946.

In 1937 the Americans began their new battleship construction programme with the two North Carolina class. It had originally been intended that these should mount twelve 14-inch guns in quadruple turrets, but the failure of the Japanese to ratify the London treaty led to a change to nine 16-inch instead, in three triple turrets. As the displacement limit had been observed, a speed of 28 knots was all that could be managed without sacrificing armour. Four South Dakota class

Japanese battleship *Yamato*.

of similar size and armament were authorised by Congress in 1939 and the final design was for six Iowa class, of 48,000 tons with nine 16-inch guns and capable of 33 knots.

Four of these joined the fleet in 1943–4, with the other two being cancelled, as were the succeeding five ships of the Montana class (60,500 tons and twelve 16-inch). Two ships of the Alaska class, completed in 1944, are variously described as large cruisers of 30,000 tons, or as battle cruisers, because of their armament of nine 12-inch. As neither saw action, and as both were laid up immediately after the war ended, the question is academic.

Under conditions of great secrecy, with the building concealed by sisal curtains, Japan built the ultimate in battleships, *Yamato* and *Musashi* of 65,000 tons and armed with nine 18.1-inch guns – a huge tender being built to carry the immense gun barrels from the ordnance factory to the dockyard for installation. A third, *Shinano*, was completed as an aircraft carrier and a fourth cancelled.

Chapter Ten

Battle Fleets in Action, 1939–45 – the North Sea and the Atlantic

W hen Britain and France responded to Germany's attack on Poland in September 1939 by declaring war, they had no way of intervening directly by land or air, and the period known as the Phoney War began. The war at sea, however, began from the first day and here the Allies had a degree of superiority even greater than in 1914. Germany had in commission only *Scharnhorst*, *Gneisenau* and the three pocket battleships. The Royal Navy, by contrast, had fifteen capital ships, though the latest refitting of *Queen Elizabeth* and *Valiant* was not quite complete. Twelve of the ships were, however, of First World War vintage despite some modernization. The most modern were the two Nelson class, already in service for twelve years. France had six old dreadnoughts and the two Dunkerque class in commission. These could be stationed in the Mediterranean against any possible threat from Hitler's ally Mussolini. Although the Pact of Steel, signed six months earlier in May 1939, had changed the Rome–Berlin Axis into a military alliance, Italy was unprepared for war and for the time being remained neutral.

The only naval strategy open to Germany was the classic recourse of the weaker power, the 'guerre de course'. In anticipation of the opening of hostilities, *Deutschland* and *Admiral Graf Spee* were already at sea in August 1939 and were able to strike at the Atlantic trade routes. *Deutschland* sank only two ships of 6,000 tons before her recall, when she was renamed *Lützow*, lest the loss of a ship named after the Fatherland should have adverse propaganda value.

Admiral Graf Spee had more success in the South Atlantic and in a brief foray into the Indian Ocean. Here ships were sailing independently and the raider picked off nine, with an aggregate of 50,000 tons. Her captain, Hans Wilhelm Langsdorff, scrupulously observed the rules of cruiser warfare: her victims were stopped by warning shots and their crews taken off before the vessels were sunk. The captains and first engineers were kept aboard *Graf Spee* while the remaining crew members were transferred to the raider's supply ship, *Altmark* from which they were eventually released (in Norwegian waters) by the destroyer HMS *Cossack*.

No fewer than eight different hunting groups were employed in the search for the German raider, including the battle cruiser HMS *Renown* and the French ships, *Strasbourg* and *Dunkerque*, all of which were faster and more heavily armoured than the *Graf Spee*. Also, there were two carriers and fourteen cruisers assigned to the task. It was Commodore Henry Harwood's three cruisers of Force G which eventually intercepted *Graf Spee* off the estuary of the River Plate and there followed a running battle. The 11-inch guns of the raider gave her a total weight of broadside double that of her opponents, but they were mounted in two turrets and she had three opponents, which attacked her from different quarters.

By concentrating her fire on the 8-inch gunned cruiser *Exeter* she was able to put out of action the most powerful of the British vessels in Force G, but sustained damage and lacked the speed to escape. Pursued by the 6-inch gunned cruisers, *Ajax* and *Achilles*, (the latter a ship of the New Zealand navy), *Graf Spee* took refuge in the neutral port of Montevideo, capital of Uruguay.

Intense naval and diplomatic activity followed Captain Langsdorff's request for time to be allowed for the repair of his ship. While British opposition to the completion of any but essential repairs outwardly suggested the desire for the warship to put to sea again as soon as possible, the sailing of a series of British merchant vessels was arranged to delay her departure. International law decreed that twenty-four hours had to elapse between the sailings of ships of rival belligerents from a neutral port. Meanwhile, the damaged *Exeter* had been ordered back to the Falkland Islands to be replaced by the 8-inch gunned HMS *Cumberland*. It would be some days before more substantial help could arrive. The faulty intelligence that *Renown* and the carrier *Ark Royal* had reinforced the waiting cruisers was enough to convince the Germans that it would not be possible for *Graf Spee* to return to Germany and she was scuttled in the estuary of the Plate.

If the first blood had been gained by Britain, the German surface raiders now had success. The *Admiral Scheer* attacked the convoy HX 84, escorted only by the armed merchant cruiser HMS *Jervis Bay*. The auxiliary cruiser bravely engaged the German warship, enabling the convoy to scatter, so that all but six of the merchantmen escaped.

In all *Admiral Scheer* sank seventeen victims, totalling 113,000 tons in five months at large, before returning to Kiel. Neither she nor *Lützow* were again to menace the Atlantic routes. *Scharnhorst* had also sunk an armed merchant cruiser, the P&O liner *Rawalpindi* on patrol off Iceland in 1939. In February 1941 she sailed with *Gneisenau* on a cruise commanded by Admiral Günther Lütjens, which led to the destruction of twenty-two ships, a total of 115,000 tons. That this was not larger was due to the Admiralty policy of using battleships as escorts to convoys. The German raiders three times encountered convoys escorted by capital ships and each time they refused to risk damage in action with a more heavily-armed, if slower opponent.

In February 1941 they came upon convoy HX 106, escorted by HMS *Ramillies*, and in March they fell in with a Sierra Leone convoy, escorted by another 15-inch battleship, HMS *Malaya*. Similarly they found convoy SL 67 protected by the 16-inch HMS *Rodney*. The old, unmodernised battleships of the Revenge class were ideally suited to this work, where their lack of speed was of little disadvantage and where their 15-inch guns could deliver the kind of blow which no raider could risk taking. The destruction of the raider would be the ideal outcome, but not the sole aim: serious damage would be enough to put an end to her depredations. HMS *Ramillies* had already escorted troop convoys to France in 1939, *Resolution* and *Revenge* had protected transatlantic convoys carrying Canadian troops to England, while *Malaya* protected convoys with reinforcements for the Eighth Army in North Africa, via the Cape of Good Hope. Similar duties fell to *Nelson* and *Rodney* in 1942, and to the battle cruisers *Repulse* and *Hood*, which had the added advantage of speed.

The crucial point in the threat by surface raiders on the shipping lanes came in May 1942. The newly-completed *Bismarck*, accompanied by the 8-inch heavy cruiser *Prinz Eugen* and again commanded by Admiral Lütjens, was ordered into the Atlantic. The two ships had first been identified as they passed through the Kattegat, off Denmark, and were then spotted by RAF reconnaissance aircraft in Korsfjord, Norway. The Norwegian resistance and Fleet Air Arm reconnaissance then showed them to have sailed and Admiral Tovey deployed all units of the Home Fleet to cover possible routes into the Atlantic. The least likely was that to the north of Scotland, which could be watched from Scapa Flow, where a scouting force of four light cruisers was backed by *King George V* and *Repulse*, together with the carrier *Victorious*. The passage between the Faroes and Iceland was also covered by three cruisers, with HMS *Prince of Wales* and HMS *Hood* off Iceland. The most distant, and the likeliest route for Lütjens to choose, was the Denmark Strait between Iceland and Greenland where the 8-inch cruisers *Norfolk* and *Suffolk* were on patrol.

It was in the Denmark Strait that *Suffolk* sighted the German ships, keeping them under observation by radar while she was joined by *Norfolk*, and then by *Hood* and *Prince of Wales*. Soon after dawn on 24 May, *Hood* opened fire on the leading German vessel *Prinz Eugen*, while *Prince of Wales* correctly identified *Bismarck* and also opened fire. The British ships, approaching at a shallow angle, could only use their forward turrets. The range was closing slowly when both German ships targeted *Hood*. It is now thought by some that an 8-inch shell from *Prinz Eugen* hit the lightly protected 4-inch guns magazine and the explosion penetrated to the main 15-inch magazine. *Hood* was destroyed as suddenly as her predecessors had been at Jutland. Only three members of the crew survived; 1,415 men on board lost their lives.

The newly-commissioned *Prince of Wales*, already experiencing trouble with B turret, was now the target for both German ships, had five of her ten 14-inch guns put out of action. She was also severely hit as she turned away to break off the engagement.

She had, however, caused damage to *Bismarck* leading to a leak of oil fuel and seawater contamination to her fuel tanks. This damage combined to lead Lütjens to decide that he must abandon the enterprise, and make for Brest, where there was a dry dock capable of taking a ship the size of *Bismarck* to enable repairs to be made. *Prinz Eugen* was

HMS *Prince of Wales*.

detached to make her own way to safety, while *Prince of Wales* remained in support of the covering cruisers. Admiral Sir John 'Jack' Tovey left Scapa Flow with his main force, at the same time detaching other ships to join the hunt – these included *Rodney*, *Ramillies* and *Revenge* as well as Force H from Gibraltar. An attack by Swordfish torpedo bombers from *Victorious* scored one hit, but failed to stop the battleship which then contrived to elude the shadowing cruisers during the night. A sighting by a Catalina of RAF Coastal Command regained contact, and another strike from *Ark Royal*'s Swordfish succeeded in achieving two torpedo hits. One, amidships, caused little damage, but the second hit the rudder and made the ship unmanoeuverable. *Bismarck* survived determined destroyer attacks during the night, but *King George V* and *Rodney* were within range at dawn and she was first crippled by gunfire, and a torpedo hit from *Rodney* (an event unique in the age of the battleship) and then sunk by a torpedo by the cruiser *Dorsetshire*. Even then her surviving crew member claimed that she had been scuttled, giving rise to claims that she and her sister were unsinkable.

Whatever the truth of such assertions, and despite the blow she had struck by the sinking of *Hood*, the inescapable fact was that *Bismarck* was gone, and with her the threat from surface ships to the Atlantic trade routes. This was only the first stage of the battle of the Atlantic, but from this point it was to be the submarine which posed the main threat, and it was the escort group – destroyers, corvettes and eventually the escort carrier and long-range aircraft – which was to combat that threat. Battleships were to be deployed less frequently in the Atlantic, though in August 1941 *Prince of Wales* took Mr Churchill to Newfoundland for a meeting with President Roosevelt, escorting a convoy home, while *Duke of York*'s first operation was also as escort to a convoy in December of that year. By that time, the Americans were mounting Neutrality Patrols which involved *Texas*, *New York* and *Arkansas*, while after her entry into the war, *Mississippi*, *New Mexico* and *Idaho* were also employed as escorts.

Prinz Eugen had successfully evaded the British ships after parting company from *Bismarck* and had joined *Scharnhorst* and *Gneisenau* in Brest. There the air attacks, which had already inflicted enough damage to prevent the battle cruisers from joining *Bismarck* in her foray, continued. Eventually Admiral Otto Ciliax was ordered to risk the hazardous passage of the direct route through the Channel to bring the three ships back to the relative safety of a German port. This, aided by a series of accidents and the slow reaction of the British, he contrived to do. After fighting off successive attacks by motor torpedo boats, Swordfish torpedo bombers of the Fleet Air Arm, and Hudsons and Beauforts of the Royal Air Force, both *Scharnhorst* and *Gneisenau* struck mines off the Dutch coast. They reached the safety of Wilhelmshaven and Brunsbüttel respectively, but were in need of substantial repair. *Gneisenau* never put to sea again. Their presence, together with *Lützow* and *Admiral Scheer* as well as *Tirpitz*, threatened the Arctic supply convoys to Murmansk and Archangel which began in August 1941, following Hitler's attack on the Soviet Union. It was therefore necessary for the Admiralty to retain two modern battleships and a carrier at Scapa Flow to counter this menace. They were supported in this task by USS *Washington* in 1942, and in the following year by the *Alabama* and *South Dakota*. The battleships were deployed as distant cover to the convoys, being kept to the west of the narrow channel between the north of Norway and the edge of the Arctic ice. Cruisers were employed as the main cover, with a close escort of destroyers, anti–aircraft ships and escort carriers.

An operation involving *Tirpitz*, *Lützow*, and *Scheer* was planned against convoy British convoy PQ17. The Admiralty ordered the escort to leave and the convoy to scatter. The surface threat did not materialise, but the merchantmen were defenceless against the onslaught of submarines and of aircraft flown from bases in Norway. It was a disaster, only ten of thirty-three merchantmen reached Murmansk. The battleships *King George V* and *Washington* were too far to the west to be involved. The same was true of *Duke of York* and *Anson* when PQ18 was attacked in September 1942.

The success of the escorting destroyers and cruisers, in driving off the attacks by *Lützow* and the 8-inch cruiser *Admiral Hipper* on the convoy JW51B in December 1942, had far-reaching effects. Hitler, infuriated by the failure, told Admiral Raedar of his 'firm and unalterable resolve' to decommission all the capital ships whose guns would be used to equip coastal batteries and whose crews would be redeployed. This precipitated Raeder's resignation, and his replacement by Admiral Karl Dönitz, but the big ships were retained. Dönitz was able to convince Hitler that the work of breaking up the ships was too lengthy and involved too big a task for Germany to undertake at that stage of the war.

Scharnhorst and *Tirpitz* were the two most powerful of the German warships, and both became major targets for British forces. An assault on the great Normandie dock at St Nazaire had already been carried out to deny *Tirpitz* the one major repair yard which would have enabled her to operate in the Atlantic. Now that she was based in a Norwegian fjord, she was the object of a daring attack by midget submarines. Towed across the North Sea, three of these X-craft penetrated the net defences around the battleship; the explosions of the charges which they placed beneath her hull put her out of action for six months. She was therefore unable to accompany *Scharnhorst* on her attack on convoy JW55B and the returning RA55A in December 1943. Intercepted by the cruisers of Rear Admiral Sir Robert Burnett, *Scharnhorst* was brought within the range of the 14-inch guns of HMS *Duke of York*, and sunk off North Cape.

Tirpitz was the target of repeated air attacks, first by aircraft of the Fleet Air Arm and then by the Royal Air Force. Finally, in November 1944, she was overwhelmed by 12,000 pound Tallboy bombs dropped by Lancasters of 9 and 617 Squadrons. She capsized and sank in Tromso Fjord, never having fired her great guns in action.

HMS *Duke of York*.

Battleships had also been used in home waters in support of military operations. The German invasion of Norway in 1940 had seen the deployment of the two battle cruisers which were involved in action: HMS *Renown* along with the *Gneisenau* suffering damage, the latter being torpedoed by the submarine HMS *Clyde*. *Scharnhorst* sank the carrier HMS *Glorious*, but was then struck by a torpedo from the destroyer HMS *Acasta*. Both German ships were under repair for some months, along with *Lützow*, hit by coastal batteries and later torpedoed by the submarine HMS *Spearfish*. The heavy German cruiser *Admiral Hipper* also needed dockyard attention after her unequal duel with the destroyer *Glowworm*. The Germans also lost the 8-inch cruiser *Blucher* to coastal batteries, and two light cruisers: *Königsberg* to dive bombers of the Fleet Air Arm and *Karlsruhe* torpedoed by the submarine HMS *Truant*. Ten destroyers were sunk at Narvik, where HMS *Warspite* was in support during the second of the two battles.

This rendered the German navy virtually non-existent at the time of the hastily-prepared Operation Sealion, the projected invasion of Britain. While air superiority was the first requirement, which was, of course, never achieved, there would have been quite inadequate naval escort for any seaborne invasion force. Such an assault would have faced attack by *Nelson*, *Rodney* and *Repulse* from Scapa Flow, with *Valiant*, *Barham*, *Resolution*, and *Renown* at Gibraltar. How these would have fared against air attack in confined waters is imponderable, but certainly the success of such an invasion would not have been as assured as has often been suggested.

HMS *Royal Oak*. (© *National Maritime Museum, Greenwich, London*)

The British ships had not escaped unscathed in the first year of war. HMS *Nelson* had been mined off Scotland in December 1939 and did not rejoin the fleet until the following August. In the same month *Barham* was torpedoed by U-30 off the Clyde and was in dock until April 1940. *Rodney* had been hit by a bomb which failed to explode, and *Malaya* was torpedoed by U-106 off Cape Verde while escorting a convoy, but all of these survived. Less fortunate was *Royal Oak*, torpedoed and sunk at her mooring in Scapa Flow by U-47. An old and unmodernised ship, she was of limited value, but her destruction and the loss of over 800 crew in what was thought to be a secure anchorage, was a blow to morale. Two of her 15-inch turrets were salvaged and were used to arm the monitors *Abercrombie* and *Roberts*, designed for coastal bombardment.

The surviving German pre-dreadnoughts *Schliessen* and *Schleswig-Holstein* had bombarded the Polish port of Gdansk in the opening days of the war, while *Lützow* and *Scheer* shelled Soviet positions in the campaigns of 1944–5. All four of these ships, together with *Gneisenau*, were heavily damaged by air attacks in the closing months of the war, and sank in shallow waters. By the time of Hitler's death his battle fleet had ceased to exist.

The Allies were able to deploy units of their battle fleets in support of the Normandy landings and subsequent operations. *Warspite, Rodney, Nelson, Ramillies*, together with USS *Arkansas, Texas* and *Nevada* were part of Operation Neptune, the naval operation on D-Day, while *Malaya* saw her final action off St Malo in December 1944. With the balance in the war at sea, it now proved possible to send the more modern ships out to the Pacific, to lay up *Revenge* and *Resolution* and to lend *Royal Sovereign* to Russia. Renamed *Archangelsk*, she served with the Soviet navy until 1949. Of the two old French battleships interned in English ports during the war, *Paris* had been an accommodation ship at Plymouth, while *Courbet* was sunk along with the old target ship *Centurion* as part of the breakwater for the Mulberry Harbour.

Chapter Eleven

War in the Mediterranean

In the North Sea and in the Atlantic, the battleship had continued to play a significant part in the struggle for command of the seas, even though the impact of both land and carrier-based aircraft had led to vital revision of long-held views. Air reconnaissance in the early stages of the *Bismarck* operation and the torpedo strike which finally prevented her escape; the pounding of the battle cruisers first at Brest, and later at Kiel, and the sinking of *Tirpitz*, had all proved the need to take into account a new dimension in naval warfare. It was to be very much the same story in the Mediterranean. Here the French fleet, based at Toulon and at Mers-el-Kebir, was to control the western part of that sea and to counter the possible use of a comparable Italian fleet should Mussolini decide to enter the war. The Royal Navy's Mediterranean bases were still at Gibraltar, Malta and Alexandria, but the proximity of Italian air bases in Sicily made it doubtful whether Malta would remain tenable. In 1939 only two battleships, *Barham* and *Malaya*, were attached to the Mediterranean Fleet and at the turn of the year both were temporarily withdrawn for duties elsewhere.

In mid-1940 the collapse of France and the entry of Italy into the war changed the entire Admiralty strategy in the Mediterranean. The Italian fleet included four old, but modernised battleships, along with the new 15-inch gunned *Littorio* and *Vittorio Veneto* almost ready for combat, in addition to substantial numbers of smaller craft. While Italy had no aircraft carrier, she expected to be able to dominate the central basin of the Mediterranean with land-based aircraft.

When France fell, therefore, Britain was faced not only with the need to fight on alone, but also with the possibility that units of the French fleet might be deployed against her. Two of France's older battleships, *Courbet* and *Paris* were based on Cherbourg and Brest respectively, and they made their way to internment in British ports in June 1940. The third, *Ocean* (originally named *Jean Bart*) was at Toulon as a training ship. *Lorraine* was at Alexandria, where she too was interned, but her two sisters, *Bretagne* and *Provence* were at the north African base of Mers-el-Kebir near Oran, together with the modern battle cruisers *Dunkerque* and *Strasbourg*. Not yet in service were the newest 15-inch battleships *Richelieu* and *Jean Bart*, the former at Brest and the latter at Saint Nazaire. Just before the Germans overran northern France, *Richelieu* was transferred to Dakar in Senegal, while the incomplete *Jean Bart* was taken to Casablanca on the Atlantic coast of Morocco.

The Admiralty now deployed *Warspite, Barham, Ramillies*, and *Royal Sovereign* to Alexandria under Admiral Cunningham, and created a new Force H based at Gibraltar under Vice-Admiral Sir James Somerville. This initially comprised the battle cruiser *Hood*, the battleships *Valiant* and *Resolution* and the carrier *Ark Royal*, together with cruisers and destroyers. The first duty of Force H was to ensure that the ships at Oran should not fall into enemy hands. Somerville was to offer five alternatives to Admiral Marcel-Bruno Gensoul, any of which would satisfy British requirements, but none was acceptable to the French. Three in fact, either directly or indirectly, contravened the terms of France's armistice with Germany: that Gensoul's squadron should either put to sea to continue the fight alongside their former ally, or that they should sail with reduced crews to a British or a French West Indian port for internment. They could be scuttled or demilitarised, failing which they would be destroyed by gunfire. The demands added further humiliation to a defeated, but proud nation, whose leaders were also concerned about the possibility of German reprisals. After a final warning that if none of the alternatives was accepted, the French ships would be destroyed, the British opened fire. *Bretagne* blew up, *Provence* and *Dunkerque* were crippled, while *Strasbourg* contrived to get under way and, despite attacks from torpedo bombers from *Ark Royal*, reached Toulon.

Richelieu was attacked in harbour at Dakar by torpedo bombers from HMS *Hermes*, which inflicted damage additional to that caused by a depth charge placed under her stern by daring assailants in a motor boat. Later still, she fought off an attack by *Barham* and *Resolution*, during which a French submarine scored one torpedo hit on *Resolution*.

Eventually, after the liberation of the French North African colonies, *Richelieu* went over to the Free French forces. After repairs in the New York Navy Yard she served alongside the Royal Navy with the Home Fleet in early 1944 and then in the Pacific. *Jean Bart* remained at Casablanca throughout the war, using her single turret to fight off an attack by USS *New York* and *Texas* in November 1942. She was not finally commissioned until 1955. *Dunkerque* and *Provence* were repaired and taken to Toulon where they remained until November 1942. Then, when the allied attack upon French North Africa had led to the occupation of Vichy France, they, along with *Strasbourg* and *Ocean*, were scuttled by their own crews. It is perhaps a shade incongruous that, after all the ill-feeling which the action at Oran had caused, the French ships should have all met fates in line with one or other of the British demands.

It was therefore only the Italian surface fleet which confronted Admiral Andrew Cunningham in the Mediterranean, though German and Italian aircraft and submarines were to deal some telling blows. Despite the Italian ships being more modern, faster and more numerous, they were not handled offensively enough and the initiative usually lay with the British fleet. An early indication came less than a week after the action at Oran, when *Warspite* found herself in action with the Italian battleships *Giulio Cesare* and *Conti di Cavour*. A single 15-inch shell struck the Italian flagship, at a range of thirteen miles, and was enough to make the Italian ships turn away before *Warspite*'s slower consorts, *Malaya* and *Royal Sovereign*, could come within range.

An even more unequal encounter eighteen months later in the Gulf of Sirte resulted in the repulse of an Italian force. This included the new battleship *Littorio*, the rebuilt *Andre Doria* and *Giulio Cesare*, two cruisers and ten destroyers. Force K was commanded by Admiral Sir Philip Vian and comprised light cruisers and destroyers. Both of these actions arose from the use of capital ships as escorts to convoys, a major role in the Mediterranean. The need for the Italians to resupply the Axis forces in Libya, and the priority given by Britain to convoys to Malta gave rise to much of the naval activity in the central basin.

Both convoy routes were vulnerable, but the British success in keeping Malta in operation was ultimately the crucial factor. For almost three years the island was assailed by Axis aircraft flying from bases in nearby Sicily, while relief convoys ran the gauntlet of aircraft and submarines. The convoys were escorted from Gibraltar by naval vessels including battleships, but these could not be risked beyond the Narrows so that cruisers, destroyers and carriers bore the brunt of the attacks and suffered the losses. The fighter aircraft flown off the decks of the old carriers *Eagle* and *Argus*to Malta, and the vital supply of ammunition, food and oil by the merchant ships of Operation Pedestal in August 1942 proved to be the turning point. For Operation Pedestal, a British strategy to get desperately needed supplies to the island of Malta in August 1942, *Nelson* and *Rodney* as well as the new carriers *Victorious* and *Indomitable* were deployed, but again the threat from the Italian capital ships failed to materialise. Though attacked by submarines, aircraft and E-boats in the later stages of the passage, and despite heavy losses of escorts and merchantmen, four freighters and one tanker reached Malta with just sufficient supplies to keep the island in action.

The importance of air power had been obvious from the opening of the war in the Mediterranean. While the Axis forces could deploy land-based aircraft, Admirals Cunningham and Somerville needed carriers. At first only *Ark Royal*, based on Gibraltar with Force H was available; she had at times to be deployed in the Atlantic, as in the operation against Bismarck. In September 1940 the new carrier *Illustrious* was added to Cunningham's fleet along with the modernised battleship *Valiant* and both, along with the flagship *Warspite*, were soon used to inflict a crippling blow on the Italian fleet. Reconnaissance in November 1940 showed all six of the Italian battleships to be in their main fleet base at Taranto. HMS *Illustrious* flew off a striking force of twenty-one Swordfish torpedo bombers which, despite the harbour anti-aircraft batteries, balloon barrage, anti-torpedo nets and the guns of the ships themselves, sank three of their targets.

For the loss of two obsolescent aircraft, half of the Italian battle fleet had been put out of action. In the shallow water of the harbour they had sunk to the level of their main decks and could be raised, but *Littorio* and *Caio Duilio* were out of action for six months after receiving three hits and one respectively. One hit was enough to end the career of *Conti di Cavour* altogether. Though raised in July 1941 and taken to Trieste for repairs, these were still incomplete when Italy signed the armistice in 1943. She was again sunk at her moorings by the Italians.

Fairey Swordfish torpedo bomber.

Raised again by a German salvage crew, she was again heavily damaged and sunk, this time finally, during an American air raid in February 1945.

HMS *Illustrious* was seriously damaged by German dive-bombers in January 1941, and departed for a major refit in an American yard, but Cunningham had her sister ship *Formidable* along with *Warspite, Valiant* and *Barham* for his next strike. In March 1941, *Vittorio Veneto*, with a force of cruisers and destroyers, was sighted first by reconnaissance aircraft from *Formidable* and then by a light cruiser squadron under Admiral Henry Pridham-Whippell. Attacked both by land-based aircraft from Crete and by *Formidable*'s Swordfish, the battleship suffered a torpedo hit aft which caused flooding and a list to port which brought her temporarily to a standstill.

By the time the next Swordfish strike took place, she was making thirteen knots and was protected by a screen of three 8-inch gun cruisers on each beam. One of these, *Pola*, took a torpedo intended for *Vittorio Veneto*, and her two sisters, *Zara* and *Fiume* were ordered to stand by her. In the night action which followed, *Valiant*'s radar detected the two escorting cruisers, which were crippled by 15-inch fire at short range. *Fiume* sank almost at once, and then *Zara* and *Pola* were sunk by the torpedoes launched by British destroyers, which also accounted for two Italian destroyers. The damaged battleship made good her escape, being capable of a better speed than the shadowing force had assumed, and the cruisers also lost touch. Even so, a considerable victory had been won, by a combination of air power, the use of radar and gunnery, without a single hit suffered by any of the British ships involved. The Italian fleet was even less inclined to risk action thereafter.

The apparent supremacy won by the Royal Navy, in the first nine months of the war in the Mediterranean, began to look very frail during the next nine. With the increased German activity in that theatre of war came an intensified use of submarines and aircraft, and in the fierce fighting around Crete, serious naval losses were suffered.

Three cruisers were sunk and five damaged, with six destroyers lost and another six damaged. Among the battleships, *Queen Elizabeth* and *Barham* were both struck by bombs, while *Warspite* was so seriously damaged by air attack that she had to be patched up and then sent to the US Navy yard at Bremerton for extensive repair. She did not return to the Mediterranean until 1943. (During this period also, the two former American battleships, now in the Greek Navy, and renamed *Kilkis* and *Lemnos* were also sunk by German dive-bombers.)

The deployment of ten German U-boats led to the loss of *Ark Royal* off Gibraltar and the sinking of *Barham* in the Eastern Mediterranean, both in November 1943. Struck by three torpedoes, the battleship began to capsize, and then blew up and sank with heavy loss of life. The spectacular sinking was captured on film and has been regularly shown since. It is thought that an explosion in an inadequately protected 4-inch magazine set off the main 15-inch magazine.

Next, *Queen Elizabeth* and *Valiant* were attacked in harbour at Alexandria by Italian 'charioteers'. Launched from the submarine *Scire* outside the boom defences of the harbour, the two-man crews of these manned underwater torpedoes penetrated the defences and attached their explosive charges to the two battleships and a tanker. All three sank in water so shallow that Italian reconnaissance failed to register the damage, but both were out of action pending extensive repair, again in American yards. This could not have happened at a worse time, coinciding as it did with the Japanese offensive in the Pacific. For the moment there were no British battleships in the Eastern Mediterranean, though the damage caused to *Vittorio Veneto* by a torpedo from the submarine *Urge*, also in December 1941, put her in dock for several months and went some way to restoring the balance.

An increasing shortage of fuel oil, combined with the reluctance to risk their capital ships meant that the Italians failed to take advantage of their numerical superiority. After being driven away by Admiral Sir Philip Vian off Cape Sirte in December 1941, they were not again used against the Malta convoys, nor were they able to cover the transport to North Africa of the supplies needed by the Axis forces there. Finally, they were not deployed against the Allied invasions directed first against French North Africa, then against Sicily and finally against the Italian mainland. The only other action which they saw was against their former allies. German bombers attacked the Italian ships on their way to Malta, after the capitulation of their country in 1943. The newest ship, *Roma*, had seen no action since entering the fleet a year earlier, but she was now sunk by a Fritz X glider bomb. *Littorio* (now renamed *Italia*) was also hit, but survived, along with *Vittorio Veneto*, to reach Malta. Both were then taken to Alexandria for internment and were anchored in Lake Amaro, at the southern end of the Suez Canal. The older *Caio Duilio*, *Andrea Doria* and *Guilio Cesare* remained in Malta.

The remaining duty performed by the British ships in the Mediterranean was that of shore bombardment in support of the Allied landings. This had first been directed, by *Warspite, Barham, Valiant* and *Ramillies* against the Libyan port of Bardia in August 1940, and then in the following January, when *Warspite, Valiant* and *Barham* shelled Valona during the Italian invasion of Albania. Tripoli also came under attack from *Warspite* and *Barham* in April 1941, after Admiral Cunningham had successfully opposed a suggestion that *Barham* be sunk there as a blockship. *New York* and *Texas* were deployed in support of the landings in French North Africa. It was felt that American ships might be less likely to meet resistance than British, with the memories of Oran still fresh, but they came under fire from *Jean Bart* and there was a good deal of action involving lighter craft.

Nelson, Rodney, Warspite and *Valiant* supported the allied forces which landed in Sicily on 10 July 1943, while the 15-inch guns of the monitors *Erebus, Abercrombie* and *Roberts* covered the crossing of the Straits of Messina eight weeks later. When the decision was taken to land another force at Salerno, well behind the Axis lines, *Warspite* and

HMS *Warspite*.

Valiant were again in support. Both came under heavy aerial attack and *Warspite* was hit by a Fritz X guided bomb which caused such damage that she had to be towed to Malta, and subsequently returned to England for repair.

With the surrender of the Italian fleet, the naval war in the Mediterranean was virtually over, and USS *Texas*, *Arkansas* and *Nevada* met no opposition when they gave support to the landings in the south of France a year later.

Chapter Twelve

Battleships in the Pacific

In European waters aircraft had already massively affected the war and would continue to do so. Air reconnaissance had revealed the location of *Bismarck* after the shadowing cruisers had lost contact and an air strike had slowed her so that the encircling surface vessels could close and sink her. Eventually her sister ship *Tirpitz* was to be crippled and then sunk by land-based Lancaster bombers. But it was in the Mediterranean that the blueprint for carrier-based strikes was to be revealed. The crippling of three Italian battleships in their defended base at Taranto, by a handful of obsolescent and slow Swordfish torpedo bombers, was an object lesson in the effective use of naval air power, which would be particularly significant in the vast spaces of the Pacific.

The Japanese, limited in battleship strength by the Washington Treaties, had begun to create a carrier force with purpose-built aircraft and to devise a new strategy for its use. It was to alter radically the war in this theatre, where the vast distances involved meant the there was no possibility that land-based air power alone could determine events. Both America and Japan had given attention to the building of carriers and to the development of a separate naval air service, though the Japanese had a far clearer idea of how they would make use of the weapon. In the US Navy there was still a powerful battleship lobby and some distrust of the claims of naval aviation.

The original experimental carriers USS *Langley* and the Japanese *Hosho* were given support roles as an aircraft transport and a training ship respectively, but each navy had seven fleet carriers in commission in December 1941, with more under construction. After the conversion of

Admiral Yamamoto.

Lexington and *Saratoga*, the Americans had built two smaller carriers, *Ranger* and *Wasp* in the 1930s, and three ships of the Yorktown class between 1937 and 1941. Eleven more (the Essex class) were on order, but the first of these was not in commission until late 1942. To their early conversions of *Akagi* and *Kaga* the Japanese had added the small *Ryujo* in 1933; while *Hiryu* and *Soryu* joined the fleet in 1939 and *Shokaku* and *Zuikaku* by 1941. Further Japanese building was for the conversion of liners, oilers and tenders, eight in all, so that they would quickly fall behind the Americans.

In 1941, the American Pacific Fleet, based at Pearl Harbor in the Hawaiian Islands, had eight battleships on its strength, as well as three fleet carriers. The Japanese Admiral Yamamoto had devised a plan of a surprise air strike by a carrier task force, to knock out this fleet and gain the initiative in the Pacific.

He warned his government that the industrial might of the USA would lead to a recovery, but that he could hope to achieve mastery of the sea for a year or eighteen months. In December 1941, therefore, a task force comprising six fleet carriers, escorted by the battleships *Kirishima* and *Hiei*, with three cruisers and nine destroyers, was clandestinely on its way. Meanwhile diplomatic activity indicated the steadily worsening relations between the two powers. Eventually problems with decoding delayed any formal declaration of war until after news of the attack had reached Washington, leading President Roosevelt to brand 7 December 1941 as 'a day that will live in infamy'.

The aerial attack was timed for 8am on a Sunday morning with the fleet base in a peacetime mode, no hint of impending war having been received, though warning messages were on the way. Admiral Chuichi Nagumo, commanding the task force, dispatched an initial strike force of 140 aircraft (forty-nine bombers, fifty-one dive bombers and forty torpedo bombers) escorted by forty-three fighters, followed by a second wave of 171. Their targets, in order of priority, were the American carriers, then the battleships, the oil storage tanks and the aircraft at the three airfields. As it happened, the American carriers were not in harbour at the time of the attack, so that the battleships became the prime targets.

In the first attack, *California*, *West Virginia*, and *Oklahoma* suffered torpedo hits: *Oklahoma* capsized and sank, as did the old target ship *Utah*, torpedoed by the second wave of 'Kate' torpedo bombers, which also crippled *Nevada*. ('Kate' and 'Val' were Allied reporting names for the bombers.) In the subsequent attacks by 'Val' dive-bombers, *Arizona* blew up, and *Maryland*, *Pennsylvania* and *Tennessee* were all struck. All eight American battleships were therefore out of action for the immediate future, though only *Arizona* and *Oklahoma* were total losses. The other ships were repaired, and in some cases almost completely rebuilt, but it was months before any of them rejoined the fleet. Admiral Nagumo's failure to launch a second strike, and destroy the machine shops and the oil tanks, meant that the victory was less complete than it might have been.

Having put the American battle fleet out of the reckoning, a further Japanese strike three days later accounted for the new British battleship *Prince of Wales* and the old battle cruiser *Repulse*. They should have been accompanied by the fleet carrier *Formidable*, but she had been damaged by grounding so, lacking effective air cover, they were discovered by Japanese land-based bombers off the coast of Malaya. First *Prince of Wales* was crippled, her steering wrecked and her anti-aircraft turrets immobilised. *Repulse* was skilfully handled, avoiding

HMS *Repulse*.

both bombs and torpedoes from the first two strikes, but a third well-co-ordinated attack first damaged her steering, and three torpedo hits sank her.

Prince of Wales, unable to defend herself, soon followed. At Pearl Harbor the American battleships had been stationary and not (so they thought) at war. Here were ships under way, their turrets manned, and yet they succumbed. It appeared that the argument, which had raged since General Mitchell's aircraft had sunk the *Ostfriesland*, had now been settled.

A small American, British, Dutch and Australian cruiser force was next overwhelmed in the Java Sea and Japan controlled the Pacific, overrunning French Indo-China, the Dutch East Indies, the Philippines, Hong Kong, Singapore and Malaya, giving them resources including rice, oil and rubber to support their war effort. Their invasion forces, escorted by the four Kongo class battleships and by heavy cruisers, enabled them to pick their targets. By this time France and the Netherlands were already under German occupation and Britain fighting for survival; none could give much support to their far eastern assets.

The Japanese mastery of the Pacific turned out to be much more short-lived than Yamamoto had expected. The American carriers had been absent from Pearl Harbor, *Saratoga* on the Pacific coast, while *Lexington* and *Enterprise* had been delivering aircraft for the defence of Midway and Wake islands. Their survival meant that they were now the focal point of the fight back, with battleships reduced to escort duties and shore bombardment.

An American counter offensive began with the battle of the Coral Sea in early 1942. The Japanese attempt to extend their perimeter by taking Port Moresby in New Guinea and threatening a strike against Australia resulted in the first-ever naval action in which the opposing fleets never made contact, all the fighting being done by the aircrews. The Japanese appeared to hold every advantage, but superior American intelligence work had made known the enemy plans. The Japanese deployed the light cruiser *Shoho*, escorted by four heavy cruisers, with the fleet carriers *Zuikaku* and *Shokaku*, similarly escorted, providing distant support. Against this were deployed the American carrier Task Force 17, spearheaded by USS *Yorktown* and TF 16 (USS *Lexington*), with cruisers necessarily providing the escort. The Japanese admiral had devised an elaborate plan to trap the Americans between his two forces, but his calculations assumed only one US carrier. The ensuing battle was a tactical draw, with the sinking of *Shoho* and the loss of forty-five aircraft and of USS *Lexington*, (thirty-six aircraft lost) and heavy damage to the *Shokaku*, but a strategic victory in that it ended the period of Japanese expansion. Perhaps equally significant was a rise in American morale, with the end of an assumption (on both sides) of Japanese invincibility.

Neither *Shokaku* nor *Zuikaku* was therefore available for the next Japanese enterprise. This was an attack on the American base on Midway Island, and again American intelligence work revealed the enemy plans, which were extremely complex and included decoy attacks on the Aleutian Islands. In all Yamamoto deployed four fleet carriers (with 260 aircraft embarked), three light fleet carriers and two seaplane carriers, with no fewer than nine battleships in support, including the newest and biggest, the 18-inch *Yamato*. Against this armada Admiral Frank Fletcher's TF17 had the carrier *Yorktown* with seventy-five aircraft, and Rear Admiral Raymond Spruance's TF16 had *Enterprise* and *Hornet* with 168 aircraft between them, and a total of eight cruisers forming the main escort. The odds were therefore more even than Yamamoto had expected; his intelligence had discounted *Yorktown* because of damage received in the Coral Sea and he was unaware of the arrival in the Pacific of *Hornet*. Again, the aircrews on both sides did all the fighting, with the result being an overwhelming American victory. They sank all four Japanese fleet carriers, *Kaga*, *Akagi*, *Hiryu* and *Soryu*, with all of their aircraft flown by the victors of Pearl Harbor. This was somewhat offset by the loss of 109 US naval aircraft, though many of the crews were rescued. No significant part was played by the Japanese battleships, though *Haruna* suffered slight damage. The balance of power in the Pacific had suddenly changed.

The Americans now began to redeploy their battleship strength, as well as introducing new carriers. By mid-1942 the refitted *Colorado*, together with *Tennessee* and *Maryland*, their damage received at Pearl Harbor repaired, were again ready for action and they were joined by the new ships *North Carolina* and *Washington*. By May 1943 the repairs to *Nevada* and *Pennsylvania* were complete, and *New Mexico*, *Idaho* and *Mississippi* were assigned to the Pacific, albeit now in the secondary role of fire support and escorts.

The subsequent battle of the Philippine Sea was known to American aviators as 'the Great Marianas Turkey Shoot', which really says it all. Again this was a battle between the aircrews, and by this time the Japanese were at a severe disadvantage. Most of their experienced crews had been lost and they were using the same aircraft types as in 1941.

F6F Hellcat fighter.

The Americans by now had the Helldiver, the Avenger torpedo bomber and the F6F Hellcat, which far outclassed their Japanese opponents.

The final confrontation in the Pacific was the battle of Leyte Gulf, fought as the Americans sought to regain the Philippine Islands. Here the largest number of warships ever deployed in a single battle faced one another. The American Third Fleet was commanded by Admiral William Halsey. Task Force 38 (Vice Admiral Marc Mitscher) comprised in all nine fleet carriers and eight light carriers, with the battleships *Iowa*, *New Jersey*, *Massachusetts* and *South Dakota*, fourteen cruisers and fifty-seven destroyers and was divided into four task groups. TF 34 was the heavy striking force under Vice Admiral Willis A. Lee, who commanded the battleships *Washington* and *Alabama* and could deploy also the four battleships of TF 38. TF 77 under Vice Admiral Thomas Kincaid comprised the battleships *Mississippi*, *Maryland*, *West Virginia*, *Tennessee*, *Pennsylvania* and the rebuilt *California*. The Japanese operation was complicated even by their standards, with four separate forces, designated Forces A & C, Carrier Force and 2nd Striking Force, and these forced actions in four different areas around the Philippines.

The first Japanese battleship loss was in the Sibuyan Sea, where the huge *Musashi* was overwhelmed by aircraft torpedoes and bombs and sank. Then in the Surigao Strait the *Fuso* was first hit by bombs and then sunk by aerial torpedoes while her sister *Yamashiro* was struck by two torpedoes from the American destroyer *Grant*, and then by gunfire from the battleships *West Virginia, Tennessee* and *California* which sank her. Off Samar the escort carriers of the Task Group 77.4 came under the fire of *Yamato* and her four supporting battleships. Two of the American escort carriers were sunk and others damaged both by gunfire and by kamikaze attacks, but they were eventually relieved by American air and surface units. These drove off the assailants, inflicting damage on *Nagato, Ise* and *Hyuga*.

In all, 282 ships had been involved and the Japanese losses had been catastrophic – four fleet carriers and their aircraft, three battleships, six heavy and three light cruisers and eight destroyers. The Americans had lost one light carrier, two escort carriers and three destroyers. Their way to the reconquest of the Philippines was open and their mastery of the Pacific complete.

The Japanese could still deploy four conventional battleships and the two battleship-carriers *Ise* and *Hyuga*. The two after-turrets in these vessels had been removed to allow a flying-off deck to operate twenty-two seaplanes to be launched by catapult and recovered by crane after landing alongside, but there is no evidence that these aircraft were ever embarked. Both ships were sunk by aerial torpedo in the Inland Sea in June 1945. *Yamato* was sunk by aerial torpedo off Okinawa, in a desperate suicide mission – she had fuel only for a one-way trip. As well as a lack of fuel, there was a lack of aircraft: the *Shinano*, sister ship of the *Yamato*, was completed as a carrier, but had no aircraft embarked when she was torpedoed and sunk by the submarine *Archerfish*.

Mutsu had already been destroyed by a magazine explosion in the Inland Sea in June 1943, and *Nagato*, survived the war only to be expended as a target vessel at Bikini Atoll in 1946. The final act was the signing of the Japanese surrender on board USS *Missouri*. There were those who thought that a carrier might have been a more appropriate location.

Chapter Thirteen

The End of the Battleship Era

After the war, there was not the problem of the disposal of the fleets of the defeated countries, which had been so acute in 1919. The capital ship strength of Germany and Japan had ceased to exist, though the breaking up of those vessels sunk in shallow waters, including *Tirpitz* in Tromso Fjord, and *Gneisenau*, *Lützow* and *Admiral Scheer* in Baltic ports, as well as the three Japanese ships sunk in the Inland Sea, continued for some years. *Nagato*, the only Japanese battleship to survive the war, was sunk at Bikini Atoll in the atomic bomb tests of 1946, along with the heavy cruiser *Prinz Eugen*, the largest German survivor.

The victors also quickly disposed of most of their ships. In Britain, all the remaining battleships were in reserve by 1955 and scrapped by 1960. The French navy discarded its two remaining ships by 1961, but the USN kept the four Iowa class in commission, employing them off Korea and Vietnam in the later wars in the Far East, and later in the Gulf.

First, however, came the cancellation of virtually all battleships, either building or on order, a recognition of the awareness that the type was obsolete, save for use in shore bombardment. In Britain these were the ships of the Lion class, two of which had been laid down in 1939 and two more were on order. Work on *Lion* and *Temeraire* was halted when it became apparent that the need for other types of ship was more urgent. A proposal in 1945 to upgrade the incomplete hulls from 40,000 to 50,000 tons with nine 16-inch guns was not implemented. The other ships, which were to have been named *Conqueror* and *Thunderer* were cancelled. Another ship, *Vanguard*, had already been launched, though she did not join the fleet until 1946. She had been laid down in 1941, and was armed with four of the well-tried 15-inch turrets taken out of *Courageous* and *Glorious* on their conversion to carriers. Of 45,000 tons, and with a secondary armament of sixteen QF 5.25-inch dual-purpose guns and no fewer than seventy-three Bofors guns of 40mm, she was, by all accounts, not only the last but also the best of her type.

The United States cancelled the last two of the Iowa class, ordered in 1942. *Kentucky* had reached a late stage in building and was in fact launched in 1950, after proposals to complete her as a missile-launching battleship were rejected, and her hull was broken up. The proposed *Illinois* had not even been laid down, though her engines had been completed and were used in other ships. The five ships of the Montana class were authorised in 1940, but were soon seen as superfluous in the new age of the fast carrier task force, and none were even laid down, the project being cancelled in 1943. Of 60,000 tons they were each to carry twelve 16-inch guns and were to have borne the names *Montana, Ohio, Maine, New Hampshire* and *Louisiana*.

Having eschewed the battle cruiser concept earlier in the century, the United States now did make plans for vessels of this type in their final ship building programme. They may be regarded as the culmination of the wartime development of the heavy cruiser, but as they mounted 12-inch guns they are often described as battle cruisers and rated as capital ships. They were to bear the names of US dependencies – *Alaska, Guam, Hawaii, Philippines, Puerto Rico* and *Samoa*, rather than the names of states, traditional in US battleships (though of course *Alaska* and *Hawaii* subsequently achieved statehood). Of these only *Alaska* and *Guam* entered service in 1944 but were broken up in 1961. *Hawaii* was launched, but never completed and her hull was broken up in 1960. The other three had been cancelled in 1943.

France had planned for two more ships of the Richelieu class, to be named *Clemenceau* and *Gascoigne*. The former was launched in 1943, but her hull was sunk by allied bombing the following year and the latter was cancelled. Two (unnamed) sisters were proposed in April 1940, but events soon overtook those plans.

Only the USSR of the victorious powers continued to contemplate further battleship construction. These were the three ships of the Sovetsky Soyuz class of 59,000 tons and with a main armament of nine 16-inch guns. Of these, the name ship was laid down in 1938, and her sisters, *Sovetskaya Belorussiya* and *Sovetskaya Ukraina*, in 1939 and 1938 respectively. Work was halted in 1940 and all three ships were disposed of by 1949, though the complexity of the Cold War prevented any detailed knowledge of any of them.

Of the British First World War vessels, four Queen Elizabeth class and four Royal Sovereign class had survived the war, along with the battle cruiser *Renown*. These were disposed of by 1949, having first given service as training or depot ships. First to go was *Warspite* which in a later era of increased awareness of history and less economic stringency, would have been a prime subject for preservation. Sold for scrap in 1946, she was being towed to a breaker's yard on the Clyde when she broke her tow in a gale and grounded in Prussia Cove near Land's End and was broken up there over the next three years. *Queen Elizabeth*, *Valiant* and *Malaya* along with *Renown* went less dramatically in 1948, as did *Ramillies*, *Resolution* and *Revenge*. *Royal Sovereign* survived one year longer, having been on loan to the USSR, where she had been known as *Arkhangelsk*. Of the newer ships, *Nelson* and *Rodney* also went to the breakers in 1948, but the King George V class remained in service until 1957. They had some training duties in reserve, before being deleted and scrapped, *Vanguard* following them in 1960. All that remains are the two gigantic 15-inch barrels outside the Imperial War Museum, one saved from HMS *Ramillies* and the other from the monitor HMS *Roberts*, (formerly on HMS *Resolution*).

France still had in commission three ships of First World War vintage, *Ocean*, *Lorraine* and *Paris*. Though *Ocean* was broken up in

1945, the other two survived until 1953 and 1955 respectively before they too were scrapped. The wrecks of the old *Bretagne* and *Provence*, and of the battle cruisers *Dunkerque* and *Strasbourg* were broken up, leaving only the two Richelieu class in service. Of these, *Jean Bart* had been the last battleship to be completed by any navy, after being a long time in building. She had been laid down in 1936 at Saint Nazaire, and the hull was floated in the building basin in March 1940. In June she made her way, under her own steam, to Casablanca to escape from the advancing Germans where she remained there for the rest of the war. Only one of her quadruple turrets had been fitted, but she used this to fire on USS *Massachusetts* supporting the US forces invading French North Africa in 1942, but herself sustained heavy damage from 16-inch shells and bombs. Taken to Brest for completion in 1945, she was not ready for trials until 1949, nor was she complete until 1952. She was in the support force for the Suez operation in 1956, but was sold for scrap in 1962. *Richelieu* had been placed in reserve in 1956, and went to the scrapyard in 1968.

Although the Italians had ended the war on the allied side, the losses inflicted during their Axis partnership were reflected in the post-war arrangements for their battle fleet. *Littorio*, renamed *Italia*, was allocated to the USA and *Vittorio Veneto* to Britain, for scrapping in each case, while the incomplete *Impero* was broken up at Trieste where she lay. The elderly *Giulio Cesare* was handed over to the Soviet Union, serving as *Novorossiysk* until 1956. She replaced the on-loan *Resolution*. This left Italy with only *Caio Duilio* and *Andrea Doria* which remained in service as training ships until 1956.

Around the same time the remaining South American battleships were disposed of: Brazil's *Sao Paolo* sank near the Azores when on her way to the breakers in 1951, while *Minas Gerais* was scrapped in 1954. The Argentinian *Rivadavia* and *Moreno*, almost fifty years old, followed them in 1957. The last to go was the Chilean *Almirante Latorre* in 1959. She was the last survivor of Jutland, having fought there as

HMS *Canada*, before being restored to her Chilean owners after the war. The last of the First World War dreadnoughts, the Turkish *Yavuz Sultan Selim* (ex SMS *Goeben*) went as late as 1972, despite a last-minute attempt at preservation.

Three Russian dreadnoughts of the Gangut class of 1911 survived both world wars as well as two revolutions and a flurry of renaming and lasted until the 1950s. They saw little active service in either war and *Gangut* (renamed *Oktyabrskaya Revolyutsiya* in 1925) was in use as a training ship until 1959. *Marat* (ex- *Petropavlovsk*) was sunk in harbour in 1941, but remained partially afloat and was used as a gun battery. She remained in service after the war as the artillery ship *Volkhov*. *Sevastopol* (renamed *Parizhskaya Kommuna*) served in the Black Sea, reverting to her original name, but the fourth ship, originally, *Poltava*, (later *Mikhail Frunze*) was seriously damaged by fire and was cannibalised for spare parts before being scrapped in 1956.

Finally, the United States had ended the war with twenty-three battleships in commission. During the next few years she disposed of all the older (pre-1941) ships except *Texas* which was retained at San Jacinto as a museum ship. *Arkansas* was sunk at Bikini Atoll in atomic bomb tests, but *New York, Nevada* and *Pennsylvania* all survived the nuclear explosions, only to be sunk later as target ships. *Oklahoma*, deemed beyond repair after being sunk at Pearl Harbor, now sank while on tow to a breaker's yard, but *Wyoming* (a training ship throughout the war) *New Mexico* and *Idaho* were all scrapped in 1947. *Mississippi* was used as a gunnery training vessel and then for testing missile systems until 1956, when she too was deleted, to be followed by *Tennessee, California, Colorado, Maryland* and *West Virginia* in 1959. These five had been in reserve since the war, together with the South Dakota class and the North Carolina class. Three of these have been preserved, but the others (*Washington, South Dakota* and *Indiana*) were all scrapped in 1961–3, leaving only the four Iowa class in commission.

These ships were deployed as fire support ships off Korea, and then went into reserve in 1955. *New Jersey* was refitted and reactivated for similar duty off the coasts on Vietnam in 1967–9 before again being decommissioned. Then all four ships were modernised and re-equipped with Tomahawk cruise missiles and Harpoon SSMs from 1982. In this configuration, *New Jersey* and later *Iowa* saw action off

USS *Iowa* at San Francisco in drycock, 1945.

Japanese pre-dreadnought Mikasa.

Lebanon in 1983–4, an explosion in the latter ship's B turret killing fifty of her crew. *Wisconsin* and *Missouri* gave fire support in the Arabian Gulf in 1991, after which all four were decommissioned.

The remaining battleships are a rather unrepresentative selection. Apart from the four Iowas, those preserved in America owe as much to the location of their name-states as to any distinction they achieved in action. They comprise *Texas* (which joined the fleet in 1912), *North Carolina* (1941), *Massachusetts* (1942) and *Alabama* (1942). Additionally *Arizona* (1915) is preserved as a war grave at Pearl Harbor. Of the four Iowas, *Missouri* is moored as a memorial at Pearl Harbor, *New Jersey* in that state and *Iowa* at San Francisco. *Wisconsin* is at Norfolk Virginia, still nominally in reserve.

There were some missed opportunities: the preservation of *Almirante Latorre* (ex-*Canada*) would have been a link with Jutland and of *Yavuz* (ex-*Goeben*) with the Mediterranean in 1914. But the greatest loss was *Warspite*. She had been at Jutland, at Narvik and Cape Matapan, and had been fleet flagship in the Mediterranean and the Pacific, before giving fire support off the beaches of Salerno and Normandy. *Mikasa*,

Admiral Togo's flagship at Tsushima is a link with the emergence of Japan as a naval power

The other surviving battleships are relics of a much earlier age – *Victory* (1765) and *Warrior* (1860), both at Portsmouth.

Bibliography

Barnett, C., *Engage the Enemy More Closely: the Royal Navy in World War II*, Penguin Books, 2000.

Bartlett, C.J., *Great Britain and Sea Power 1815–53*, Clarendon Press, 1963.

Baxter, J.P., *The Introduction of the Ironclad Warship*, Harvard University Press, 1933.

Bennett, G., *Naval Battles of the First World War*, Pen & Sword, 2007.

Ibid., *The Battles of Coronel and the Falklands, 1914*, Pen & Sword, 2014.

Breyer, S., *Battleships and Battlecruisers, 1905–1970*, Doubleday & Company, 1973.

Breyer, S. and Thomas, K., *Battleships of the World, 1905–1970*, Conway Maritime, 1980.

Burt, R.A., *Battleships and Battlecruisers of World War One*, Seaforth Publishing, 2012.

Ibid., *British Battleships 1889–1904*, Seaforth Publishing, 2013.

Busch, F.-O., *The Sinking of the Scharnhorst*, Futura Publications, 1974.

Chesneau, R., (Ed), *All the World's Fighting Ships 1922–1946*, Conway Maritime Press, 1997.

Costello, J. and Hughes, T., *The Battle of the Atlantic*, HarperCollins Publishers, 1980.

Gardiner, R. (Ed), *All the World's Fighting Ships 1860–1905*, Conway Maritime Press, 1997.

Hamilton, C.I., *Anglo-French Naval Rivalry 1840–1870*, Clarendon Press, 1993.

Hill, J.R. (Ed), *The Oxford Illustrated History of the Royal Navy*, Oxford University Press, 1996.

Hough, R., *A History of Fighting Ships*, Octopus Books, 1975.

Ibid., *Dreadnought: the History of the Modern Battleship*, Periscope Publishing, 2003.

Ibid., *The Fleet That Had to Die*, New English Library, 1969.

Ibid., *The Hunting of Force Z*, Phoenix, 1999.

Ibid., *The Longest Battle: The War at Sea 1939–1945*, Pan Books, 1988.

Keegan, J., *The First World War*, Hutchinson, 1998.

Ibid., *The Second World War*, Pimlico, 1997.

Kennedy, P., *The Rise of Anglo-German Antagonism 1860–1914*, Humanity Books, 1987.

King, J.W., *The Warships of Europe*, Griffin, 1878.

Lewis, M., *The Navy in Transition, 1814–1865*, Hodder & Stoughton, 1965.

Lord, W., *Incredible Victory – The Battle of Midway*, Harper & Row, 1967.

Macintyre, D., *Jutland*, Macmillan, 1977.

Ibid., *The Battle of the Atlantic*, Pen & Sword Maritime, 2014.

Ibid., *The Battle for the Mediterranean*, Macmillan, 1970.

Ibid., *The Battle for the Pacific*, Batsford, 1966.

Ibid., *The Naval War Against Hitler*, Batsford, 1971.

Marder, A.J., *From the Dreadnought to Scapa Flow*, Seaforth Publishing, 2013.

Ibid., *The Anatomy of British Sea Power: A History of British Naval Policy in the Pre-Dreadnought Era, 1880–1905*, Alfred A. Knopf, 1940.

Pack, S.W.C., *The Battle of Matapan*, Pan Books, 1968.

Padfield, P., *The Battleship Era*, Pan Books, 1975.

Parkes O., *British Battleships*, Seely Service & Co., 1971.

Pope, D., *The Battle of the River Plate*, Pan Books, 1974.

Preston, A., *Battleships*, Gallery Books, 1990.

Randall, I. (Ed), *All the World's Fighting Ships 1906–1921*, Conway Maritime Press, 1997.

Ropp, T., *The Development of a Modern Navy: French Naval Policy 1871–1904*, Naval Institute Press, 1987.

Roskill, S.W., *The War at Sea 1939–45*, Naval & Military Press, 2004.

Ibid., *HMS Warspite*, Collins, 1957.

Steele, N. and Hart, P., *Jutland 1916: Death in the Grey Wastes*, Orion, 2003.

Thomas, D., The Battle of the Java Sea, Pan Books, 1971.

Tute, W., *The True Glory*, The Book Service, 1983.

Watts, A.J., *The Royal Navy: An Illustrated History*, Caxton Editions, 2000.

Von der Porten, E.P., *The German Navy in World War Two*, Pan Books, 1972.

Index